"The illustrations and descriptive storie helped me better understand certain sit parent going through the challenges of _____ book from start to finish as it will give them a parent's perspective and the confidence to help their teen get better."

— *Parent of a teenage girl who has recovered from anorexia*

"It is of real credit to both these very experienced authors that they can address the stark reality of dealing with an eating disorder so logically, creatively and with such spirit… Overall an excellent addition to the arena of eating disorder literature. Not only is this book a record of help but it is also a book that will provide parents with a record of learning that they can refer to now and in the future."

— *Pennie Fairbairn, Psychotherapist, South London and Maudsley*
NHS Foundation Trust, UK

"Written with clarity, Drs. Boachie and Jasper are masterful at choosing analogies that provide an 'aha' understanding of the concepts and struggles with treating eating disorders that they address in *A Parent's Guide to Defeating Eating Disorders: Spotting the Stealth Bomber and Other Symbolic ' roaches*. This book is likely to answer parents' questions not only ʾ to expect with regard to their child's illness and recovery reassure them about their roles and capacity to sur

— *Merryl Bear, Director, Nationaⁱ anada*

"A highly readable book that shoulᴅ nt whose child is suffering from an eating disorder. The ɔf helpful information: on eating disorders and their dangers, ɔ types of treatment available, and on the important role the family plays in supporting a young person to recovery. The descriptions of family therapy are very moving at times. The metaphors make even difficult concepts easy to understand, and I would recommend this book not only to parents, but to anyone wanting to work in the field of eating disorders."

— *Wendy Spettigue, MD, FRCPC, Associate Professor, University of Ottawa, Faculty*
of Medicine and Psychiatric Director

A Parent's Guide to

DEFEATING
EATING
DISORDERS

of related interest

Maintaining Recovery from Eating Disorders
Avoiding Relapse and Recovering Life
Naomi Feigenbaum
Foreword by Rebekah Bardwell Doweyko
ISBN 978 1 84905 815 5

One Life
Hope, Healing and Inspiration on the Path to Recovery from Eating Disorders
Naomi Feigenbaum
ISBN 978 1 84310 912 9

Beating Eating Disorders Step by Step
A Self-Help Guide for Recovery
Anna Paterson
ISBN 978 1 84310 340 0

Inside Anorexia
The Experiences of Girls and their Families
Christine Halse, Anne Honey and Desiree Boughtwood
ISBN 978 1 84310 597 8

Bulimics on Bulimia
Edited by Maria Stavrou
ISBN 978 1 84310 668 5

A Parent's Guide to
DEFEATING
EATING
DISORDERS

Spotting the Stealth Bomber and
Other Symbolic Approaches

AHMED BOACHIE AND KARIN JASPER

Foreword by Dr. Debra Katzman

Jessica Kingsley *Publishers*
London and Philadelphia

Figure 2.4 on p.32 reprinted with kind permission of The McCall Pattern Company.
Figure 3.4 on p.59 reprinted from Dubin 2000 with permission from Dale Dubin.
Figure 3.5 on p.60 reprinted from Andersen 1999 with permission from John Hopkins University Press.
Figure 3.7 on p.63 reprinted from Morris 2001 with permission from the editor.
Figure 3.8 on p.64 reprinted from Katzman *et al.* 1996 with permission from Elsevier.
Figure 8.1 on p.153 reprinted from Lask and Bryant-Waugh 1993 with
permission from the authors and Taylor and Francis.
All material from DSM-IV-TR in Appendix I reprinted with permission
from the American Psychiatric Association.
All material from ICD-10 in Appendix I reprinted with permission from the World Health Organization.

First published in 2011
by Jessica Kingsley Publishers
116 Pentonville Road
London N1 9JB, UK
and
400 Market Street, Suite 400
Philadelphia, PA 19106, USA

www.jkp.com

Copyright © Ahmed Boachie and Karin Jasper 2011
Illustrations copyright © Nadia Boachie 2011
Foreword copyright © Dr. Debra Katzman 2011

Library of Congress Cataloging in Publication Data
Boachie, Ahmed.
A parent's guide to defeating eating disorders : spotting the stealth bomber
and other symbolic approaches / Ahmed Boachie and Karin Jasper ; foreword by
Debra Katzman.
p. cm.
Includes bibliographical references and index.
ISBN 978-1-84905-196-5 (alk. paper)
1. Eating disorders in adolescence. 2. Eating disorders in children. 3.
Parenting. I. Jasper, Karin. II. Title.
RJ506.E18B625 2011
618.92'8526--dc22
2011005775

British Library Cataloguing in Publication Data
A CIP catalogue record for this book is available from the British Library

ISBN 978 1 84905 196 5

Printed and bound in the United States

From Ahmed

To my daughters Nadia, Zulaikhah, and Zaleekhah who inspire me to continue my work, and to my family for always being there to encourage me, particularly my mother Madina whose love has sustained me and without whom I would not be where I am today.

From Karin

To Sandy and Allison, for their faith, love, and humor, to my friends and family for their love, and especially to my mother Liselotte who taught me to think independently.

And together

To all the families and young people we have worked with.

"When we're in it, we can't see it. When we're out of it, we can see we were in it, but at first we don't feel easy being out of it."

Said by a group of teens recovering from eating disorders

Contents

Foreword

If you are the parent of a child with an eating disorder, you are probably worried, confused, upset, and have many unanswered questions. As a concerned parent, what can you do? Who can you talk with? How can you get help for your child? *A Parent's Guide to Defeating Eating Disorders: Spotting the Stealth Bomber and Other Symbolic Approaches* is a comprehensive and invaluable resource for parents that addresses these and other questions in a clear and comprehensive way. The authors, Ahmed Boachie and Karin Jasper, are two clinicians experienced in the eating disorders field and offer parents a sound roadmap for helping their child "defeat" these serious, life-threatening disorders. This unique new book was written for parents and contains practical advice based on scientific evidence that comes from years of clinical practice working with children with eating disorders and their families.

The book is divided into eight chapters and helps parents understand the various types of eating disorders, the recognition and diagnosis of an eating disorder, various types of treatment, including outpatient treatment, multi-family therapy and day treatment, and the recovery process. These chapters are presented with the objective of sharing knowledge in a very accessible way.

The authors use metaphors, analogies, case studies, and practical questions and answers to bring the book to life. This creative presentation also includes up-to-date research and its application in the clinical setting. This unique format guides parents, family members and those working with children suffering from an eating disorder in understanding these disorders and how they can help in the treatment. In so doing, the authors enlist and therefore empower parents to take an active role in the treatment of their child.

Ahmed Boachie and Karin Jasper should be congratulated for putting together this important book for parents. *A Parent's Guide to Defeating Eating Disorders: Spotting the Stealth Bomber and Other Symbolic Approaches* successfully promotes the creation of a supportive relationship between the child with an eating disorder and the parents, in an effort to ally themselves with the treatment and together "defeat" the eating disorder. Above all, this important resource empowers parents to meet the challenges needed to care for their child with an eating disorder.

Debra K. Katzman, MD, FRCP(C)

Dr. Debra Katzman is a Professor of Pediatrics, Head of the Division of Adolescent Medicine, Department of Pediatrics and University of Toronto, Medical Director of the Eating Disorders Program at the Hospital for Sick Children and Senior Associate Scientist at the Research Institute at the Hospital for Sick Children. Dr. Katzman is currently the President of the Academy for Eating Disorders. The focus of Dr. Katzman's research program is to understand the unique physiologic, psychological, and developmental issues in children and adolescents with eating disorders.

Acknowledgements

We thank our colleagues: Seena Grewal for listening to analogies, establishing the day hospital research, and for overall support of the project; Lucinda Kunkel for reviewing a draft and providing valuable feedback; and Marissa Beck for reading and commenting on early drafts of Chapters 2 and 3.

Many of our colleagues, administrative assistants, and staff, past and present, at both Sick Kids Hospital and Southlake Regional Health Centre, may not have contributed directly but have encouraged us through their enthusiasm for the use of metaphors and analogies in helping the families and patients we work with.

We are thankful to the originators of the family-based approach: James Lock, Daniel LeGrange, Stuart Agras, and Christopher Dare, and to Bryan Lask and Rachel Bryant-Waugh whose ideas about the stages of recovery have guided our approach. Also we thank Ivan Eisler and Pennie Fairbairn who provided training that has strongly influenced our understanding of how to help families take over management of their children's eating disorders in a multi-family group format.

We are especially grateful to Nadia, Zulaikhah, and Zaleekhah for their contributions of artwork and for their patience; to Sandy, for his generosity of spirit and material support, including the "Sailing off the edge of the world" analogy (p.124); and to Allison MacDonald, our project assistant, who brought order to chaos and worked tirelessly with humor and heart.

Preface

This book is not meant to re-invent the wheel. There are already several excellent books written by experts that provide a full understanding and management of eating disorders based on up-to-date research findings. A great number of books have helped to motivate parents to take over management of their child's illness. Our book brings a unique approach to enhancing this project, in that it uses a symbolic approach systematically to crystallize an understanding of eating disorders and crucial aspects of their treatment.

Children and teens with eating disorders think that no one understands them and find it difficult to trust anyone, which presents a major obstacle for recovery. Parents often try to calm their children's anxieties about food and weight-gain by minimizing expectations for food intake. The analogies and metaphors in our book will help parents understand eating disorders in a way that allows them to ally themselves with treatment rather than with the eating disorder. Professionals may also use the book to increase their understanding of the complex presentations of eating disorders, and thereby find it easier to explain them to parents. Children who believe that others grasp their experience find it easier to open up. They feel understood, respected, appreciated, and supported, thus decreasing guilt and improving their listening.

We hope you will find that *A Parent's Guide to Defeating Eating Disorders: Spotting the Stealth Bomber and Other Symbolic Approaches* provides an effective tool for improving the therapeutic alliance among professionals, parents, and children.

Female third person pronouns have primarily been used throughout the book, because the majority of those with eating disorders are female. However, the authors acknowledge that males are increasingly being diagnosed with eating disorders.

Chapter 1

Rationale for Analogies and Metaphors

THE 911 CALL

A young person with an eating disorder may ask for help and then deny that she wants it, like someone who has an intruder in her home and calls 911 but, when help arrives, finds that the intruder is standing at her back with a gun, forcing her to say everything is all right after all. After some time living with the illness and giving up hope of being rescued, the young person may also start thinking of the intruder as her protector, believing that it is better to live with the eating disorder than to give it up for some other coping mechanism which may not work. In this case, when a professional treats a young person with an eating disorder, the young person experiences the professional as an unhelpful or dangerous alternative to her protector, the eating disorder.

Eating disorders are unlike many illnesses. For instance, a child with pneumonia has many visible symptoms like coughing, sputum, and fever. Parents are alert for such symptoms and a single visit to a family doctor is usually sufficient for the diagnosis. The illness is easy to detect and its potential harm is obvious. Treatment, often a course of antibiotics, is straightforward and usually agreed to without argument. It is readily apparent when the illness has been defeated. Not so with an eating disorder.

Research suggests that only 2 percent of family doctors and 33 percent of pediatricians are likely to consider eating disorders as a possible diagnosis when they encounter them in their medical practice (Bryant-Waugh *et al.* 1992). One reason is that every eating disorder starts with weight preoccupation and dieting, which are normative in our society, especially among girls, but increasingly among boys. The moment at which dieting becomes disorder can slip by unnoticed, particularly since the child or teen will avoid acknowledging that she has become ill or may not know it herself. Also, eating disorder symptoms may mimic other common medical illnesses, especially in the early stages. This allows the eating disorder to become entrenched before the adults who could help the child to recover recognize it. Once it is entrenched, the child will not readily accept help.

Parents, simply by being parents, are in the best position to help their children recover. Children look to them for guidance and will accept that their parents can judge when it is important for them to do something. Even after an eating disorder is identified, though, there is no medication and no simple treatment that will cure it. There is evidence that suggests family-based therapy is the best available treatment for anorexia and may also be helpful for bulimia in children and adolescents.

When an illness is not well understood, myths and misconceptions arise to fill the gap in real understanding. This contributes to delays in the identification and treatment of the illness, which may then lead to poorer outcomes. For instance, the ideas that "only white, affluent, teenage girls suffer from eating disorders," "being in your healthy weight range means you do not have an eating disorder," "if you eat three meals a day and do not purge, you cannot have an eating disorder," "teens with anorexia do not eat candy, chocolate, or chips," and "boys do not get eating disorders," are amongst the myths and misconceptions that can contribute to delays in identification of eating disorders (Boachie and Jasper 2005).

Even after an eating disorder is suspected, myths and misconceptions can cause delays in seeking treatment. If parents believe or are told that "this is just a phase," or "you cannot die from an eating disorder," they may delay taking action, thinking there are no significant risks in waiting, but this allows the illness to take root. Another misconception is that the eating disorders consist solely of behaviour, which gives rise to the idea that changing the behaviour is all that is required for recovery; for example, with anorexia, that "if I just get her to eat, it will solve the problem," or with bulimia, that "if I can keep him out of the bathroom, it will solve the problem." While changing behaviour may be a very good start, this misconception confuses symptom improvement with a full recovery that includes emotional, psychological, and social components (Boachie and Jasper 2005).

Even after treatment has been started, there are myths and misconceptions that can interfere with recovery. For instance, unrealistic expectations are raised with the idea that "with treatment, the problem goes away quickly." Eating disorders can become chronic and are debilitating. The myth that they will go away quickly with treatment interferes with activation of the persistence and support that is needed for recovery. Treatment is expensive – in terms of money it can be more or less, depending on the availability and cost of health insurance. In terms of time, recovery from an eating disorder *always* requires a major investment of parents' time. This is not unusual in many areas involving children, for example, nursing a baby or helping a child learn to walk. This time investment is both priceless and crucial.

PARENTS ARE THE PRICELESS RESOURCE

What is the most priceless thing to human beings? Air. It's everywhere and it costs nothing. It comes to you even if you make no effort to find it. Just because we take it for granted, doesn't mean it isn't priceless.

Parents may ask: "Is there any other facility I can take my child to?" thinking that a more specialized or better hospital will be the answer. This is not the answer. It is you helping your child to eat that will make the difference. The key is your own presence and involvement, at whatever stage of the illness your child may be.

Sometimes parents may feel (or be) advised that their "adolescent with an eating disorder behaves this way to hurt their family and friends." However, the fact that it feels painful to parents does not mean the teen is intending to cause pain. In fact, the teen is keeping much of her own emotional pain a secret in order to spare her family members. A related misconception is that "only the adolescent needs support." Most discussions about eating disorders are related to the young person with the eating disorder and don't include the feelings and conflicts of the parents, but guidance and support for parents are essential for the recovery of their child. When parents become frightened or angry, or are in conflict with one another about how best to help their child, they need help to avoid becoming exhausted, immobilized, or unable to give their child a unified form of support. For instance, because an adolescent is normally in the process of forming his/her own identity, it can appear that arguments about food and body size are part of a teen's developing autonomy, when they may actually be manifestations of the authoritarian voice of the eating disorder. If one parent believes the teen is making autonomous choices about food intake and the other sees these choices as related to the eating disorder, their child will be confused, the eating disorder will find room to lodge, and the parents will soon become very tired.

Parents need to understand why they should intervene in areas where adolescents are usually trusted to make their own choices, for example, how much they eat, their physical activities, and their bathroom use. Analogies and metaphors help promote understanding of one concept through the context of another (Geary 2009), allowing us to see aspects of a situation that were previously unseen. Similarly, comedians make us laugh about things that are difficult to talk about and can help us focus on the right rather than the wrong things. With metaphors and analogies we can make eating disorders understandable, reduce parents' guilt and self-blame, and help them focus their strengths in a way that facilitates their children's recovery. Using analogies and metaphors this way is consistent with the current treatment model of family-based therapy.

Parental responsibility occurs in the context of children's rights, specifically the right to refuse treatment. Like the young person in "The 911 call" (p.17), a teen with an eating disorder may say that she does not need or want treatment. Parents may think that they should back off when they hear their child say that she feels fine and won't go to an appointment or to the hospital. However, parental responsibility means that in the context of health and safety, parents may temporarily need to suspend their childrens' rights in order to protect them.

WHEN INDIVIDUAL RIGHTS AND PARENTAL RESPONSIBILITY COLLIDE

In North America and Europe everyone has individual rights, even children. There are times, though, when parental responsibility overrides children's individual rights. Suppose it is the middle of winter. A five-year-old is wearing her favorite summer dress and says she is going outside. You don't stop her because she has her individual rights. Out she goes and you wave good-bye. Just then, a police officer drives by.

Parental responsibility takes priority over a child's individual rights. The individual rights are returned when the child is capable of making self-preserving decisions. No judge will criticize a parent who acts to protect a child whose heart is compromised.

Metaphors and analogies can also make it easier for adolescents with eating disorders to accept help. While describing to parents the effects of anorexia or bulimia on a child's vital organs naturally activates them, it does not usually activate the teen herself to eat more or to stop purging.

Doctor: "If you don't eat, your heart will stop."
Patient: "Okay."

Even though the information is true and the patient is not suicidal, nothing may change. It has no emotional impact on the teen. But analogies can bring the emotion back in and can help the teen to see herself and her behaviour from a different perspective. She may not be moved by the information about her heart if she has not eaten much of anything for months, has been taken by her parents to the emergency department several times, and has always been released because she is "stable." Not knowing that an emergency department cannot deal with anything but an immediate crisis, she may take this as a sign that there is nothing wrong with her and this will reinforce her mistaken idea that she does not need food to survive. (See "Driving with no gas" on p.62.)

Usually the teens who develop eating disorders are less risk-taking than average. They start off as girls who tend not to challenge authority, but the eating disorder gives them a willingness to risk and to be "in your face." They may underestimate the danger they are in and can crash suddenly. Even if they understand the risk, they may not appreciate the gravity of the illness.

There is also increasing evidence that those with eating disorders tend to have difficulties with "set shifting": they have difficulty displaying flexibility in the face of changing requirements. Rather than change the way they think about something when a change is required, they tend to continue to think about it in the same way instead. Analogies and metaphors may help them make cognitive shifts that they would not otherwise make themselves.

Because eating disorders are poorly understood and there are many myths and misconceptions about them, both parents and adolescents need education about them. Information is essential, but analogies and metaphors can help to improve understanding in a way that makes it easier for parents to ally with the treatment team to help their children, and for children to accept treatment.

Chapter 2

Eating Disorders as Illnesses: An Historical Perspective

Parents of a child with an eating disorder commonly hear well-meaning advice from relatives and friends to "just make the child eat." This advice is based on thinking that the child is behaving badly and therefore that parents should respond as they would if their child refused to tidy her room. It tends to reinforce parents' guilt and self-blame, so that they think all their unsuccessful efforts to "make their child eat" prove they are not good-enough parents. But an eating disorder is neither a bad behaviour nor a "lifestyle choice." Eating disorders are real illnesses. They take vulnerable young people, the vast majority of whom are girls, with unique perspectives, voices, and goals, and make them say similar things, want similar things, and do similar things. Professionals have been struggling to understand and treat eating disorders since at least the late 1800s.

We can think of eating patterns on a continuum, with balanced, appetite-responsive eating at one end and eating that has become consistently disconnected from appetite and other body signals at the other end (see Figure 2.1). What we refer to as eating disorders occupy the most extreme right positions on this continuum. In our culture, the factor most commonly motivating a disconnection between eating and appetite or body signals of hunger and fullness is feeling a need to control or minimize body weight, that is, to be thin or to avoid being fat.

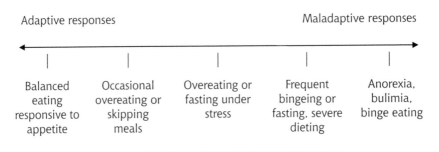

Figure 2.1: Continuum of eating regulation responses
Adapted from Cochrane 1998

Currently eating disorders are defined based on the *Diagnostic and Statistical Manual of Mental Disorders* (DSM-IV-TR) in North America, and the *International Statistical Classification of Diseases and Related Health Problems* (ICD-10) in other countries, including those in Europe. Details of these definitions are included in Appendix I.

Anorexia nervosa

In 1874 Sir William Gull, physician to the Royal Family in England, argued for the acceptance of anorexia nervosa as a discrete illness entity. He thought of it as a starving disease that could be fatal, but unlike an intestinal disease or tuberculosis, which cause difficulties in digestion or sustaining weight, anorexia has no physical basis. Nor did Gull think it to be a form of psychosis, where a person refuses to eat because of the delusion that enemies have poisoned the food supply. He saw it as rooted in the nervous system. Gull identified anorexia nervosa as affecting mostly urban girls of the upper and middle classes (Brumberg 1988), but observed that it could also affect boys. Some country girls of the time did become well known for not eating, but their parents, clergy, and physicians tended to see them as embodying a kind of miracle: as beings endowed by God with a supernatural ability to live without food.[1]

---

1   Brumberg (1988) refers to this phenomenon as *anorexia mirabilis*, the category preferred by those who did not follow the emerging domination of science at the end of the nineteenth century. Some such young women, known as "fasting girls," were exposed as frauds when they were discovered to be eating tiny amounts of food, and some died in the process of being scrutinized to determine whether they were eating anything at all.

Charles Lasegue, a French physician of the time, used the term *l'anorexie hystérique*, or hysterical anorexia (Brumberg 1988, pp.119–20), which implied that the illness had an emotional cause and affected only females. Now it is apparent that males can also develop anorexia nervosa, albeit in much smaller numbers than females. Lasegue's contribution was his description of the stages of the illness. He observed that Stage 1 is characterized by the affected girl changing her eating patterns as she expresses discomfort with eating: she feels full, or has a headache, or no longer likes the taste of some food, and begins leaving more and more foods out, while repeating others. At this time she refuses all of her parents' efforts to get her to eat, saying that she cannot eat because it makes her feel unwell. She is not yet emaciated and is still both socially and physically very active. Once the range of food she willingly eats has been reduced to almost nothing, "the disease is…declared" (Brumberg 1988, p.130).

In Stage 2, the girl says that she feels good and therefore does not need to eat. So long as she is permitted by family to eat only what she wants, she will join them at the table, but she does not take seriously any warnings that she is destroying her health and may become seriously ill. For instance, if someone points out that the girl's menses have become irregular, the girl is not concerned. At the same time, among her family members, her anorexia is the "sole object of preoccupation and conversation" (Brumberg 1988, p.131). The girl no longer takes part in activities with others, but has a "pathological contentment" (Brumberg 1988, p.132) with her situation and seems certain that she can continue to get along with only the smallest amount of food (Brumberg 1988).

In Stage 3, family and friends are aware that the girl could die. The physical impacts of starvation have become obvious, including emaciation, anemia, amenorrhea, chronic thirst, dry and pale skin, unremitting constipation, atrophied stomach, vertigo, and fainting. She spends more time lying down because exercise has come to be laborious. If parents have not previously sought medical help, most do at this stage. "The young girl begins to be anxious from the sad appearance of those who surround her, and for the first time her self-satisfied indifference receives a shock" (Brumberg 1988, p.133). Lasegue observes that at this stage the girl either becomes very obedient and eats or, more commonly, "she submits with semi-docility, with the evident hope that she will avert the peril [of death] without renouncing her ideas and perhaps the interest that her malady has inspired. The second tendency...vastly complicates the situation" (Brumberg 1988, p.133).

Bulimia nervosa

Although a few case reports of women with symptoms consistent with what we now recognize as bulimia nervosa were written between 1903 and 1945, the syndrome was not recognized, nor did it exist in large numbers, before the late 1970s. It was 1979 when Gerald Russell published an article describing it as a syndrome distinct from anorexia nervosa. It is rumored that he had been discussing cases with a dermatologist and dentist when the significance of self-induced vomiting struck him as an indication of a separate syndrome: an area of skin on the back of the hand becomes calloused, and tooth enamel is eroded by bile. Like those with anorexia, those with bulimia nervosa are also determined to control their weight, but they maintain a weight that may support menstruation. While they restrict food intake, they also experience episodes of binge-eating, which they follow with efforts to compensate for the bingeing, including self-induced vomiting, laxative or diuretic use, fasting, and over-exercise. In spite of being at normal weight, young women or men with bulimia are at risk of death because of the effects their compensating behaviours have on the body (see Chapter 3). They are also more likely than those with anorexia to abuse drugs or alcohol. Purging, along with drug or alcohol abuse, is an especially ominous prognostic factor.

Figure 2.2: The Lord of the Rings
Drawing by Nadia Boachie 2010

THE LORD OF THE RINGS

Gollum, in *The Lord of the Rings*, is a wonderful metaphor for an eating disorder. Frodo must take the Ring of Power to Mount Doom and, without succumbing to its enormous force, throw it into the molten lava below. He is traveling with his trusted friend Sam, but neither of them knows the territory they must cover. They are exhausted and weak. Gollum, who appears well-intentioned, offers to guide and protect Frodo along the hazardous route. Before long, Gollum succeeds in making Frodo so suspicious of Sam that Frodo pushes Sam away, and gives his trust totally to Gollum. Sam does not give up. When Gollum's real intention to steal the Ring becomes clear, Sam is there at the edge of the precipice to fight for Frodo and their quest. The Ring and Gollum find their end in the molten lava. (See Figure 2.2.)

Similarly, eating disorders come to young people when they are at their most vulnerable. They promise young people everything and make them disbelieve and distrust those who love them most. They need their family and friends to stay with them, even through the bitterest darkness.

27

Eating disorder not otherwise specified

There is, in fact, a spectrum of eating disorders, which share many of the same characteristics. Eating disorder not otherwise specified (EDNOS) includes the restricting symptoms of anorexia nervosa, but with normal menstruation or body mass index (BMI). It can also include the bingeing and compensating symptoms of bulimia nervosa, but with fewer weekly episodes. It is important to understand that the eating disorders in this category are serious and potentially life-threatening, just like anorexia and bulimia.

Binge-eating disorder

Binge-eating disorder is the pattern of binge-eating without the use of any compensating behaviours such as self-induced vomiting. A body of evidence is emerging that may result in a new diagnostic category being established for this eating pattern on its own. Currently, in the DSM-IV-TR, it is included under EDNOS.

What causes eating disorders?

What causes an illness that intensifies during some historical periods and occurs not at all at others; that arises in many cultures, but not in all; and that largely affects females, but can also affect males? Much has been learned about anorexia since the late 1800s, and bulimia since the 1970s, but our current level of understanding is such that most professionals today would agree there is no known cause of eating disorders.

SERIOUS ILLNESS WITHOUT A KNOWN CAUSE

Hypertension is one of the most common medical illnesses that can have devastating consequences and yet we usually do not know what causes it. Most of the time what leads up to it will be reported as unknown or primary. We know some risk factors for this illness, but we don't know the cause. Once the illness is identified, a doctor will recommend a management strategy, otherwise the patient is in danger of having severe complications, including a heart attack or severe stroke. (See Figure 2.3.)

The absence of any easily identified cause does not mean that an eating disorder is not an illness.

Figure 2.3: Hypertension: a serious illness without a known cause
Drawing by Nadia Boachie 2010

Mothers have been blamed, just as they were blamed for autism when it was first conceptualized and misunderstood to be a result of bad mothering.

NOT MOM'S FAULT

"Refrigerator mothers" was a term coined by Leo Kanner in the late 1940s to describe mothers who were thought to be so cold and uncaring that their children were traumatized and retreated into autism. Dr. Bernard Rimland, a psychologist with an autistic son, is credited with debunking this myth. Today, the bad mother view has been refuted and recent research suggests that autism is strongly related to genetics (Rudy 2006).

Eating disorders are *not* caused by a particular kind of parenting. They are complex illnesses and many factors contribute to increased risk.

Parents of a child with an eating disorder would do anything in their power to prevent it, and would pay any amount of money to change it. But an eating disorder is not parents' fault and recovery cannot be purchased. Christopher Dare and his colleagues at the Maudsley Hospital developed a treatment based on the understanding that families are not to blame for the development of an eating disorder. Instead, the Maudsley model of treatment sees the family as the most important resource in their child's recovery (Lock and LeGrange 2001). We know there are many factors that contribute to increased risk for eating disorders, but we do not know what causes them.

Risk factors: cultural conditions

A culture must give substantial meaning to a practice for there to be significant numbers of people who participate in it. For instance, in the Middle Ages in Europe, the Church gave a very positive meaning to extreme ascetic practices, especially for women. Women could become saints through the practice of intense bodily deprivation. Such women sought "[t]o obliterate every human feeling of pain, fatigue, sexual desire, and hunger..." (Bell 1985, p.20) to make themselves more spiritually perfect and therefore more pleasing to God. Catherine of Siena was one such female saint, termed by the historian Rudolph Bell a "holy anorexic" (Bell 1985, p.20). When the recognition of female saints later became attached to the accomplishment of good works rather than the "accomplishment" of withstanding deprivation, the phenomenon of "holy anorexia" largely disappeared (Bell 1985, p.190). In a contemporary variation on this theme, a study in Ghana (Bennett *et al.* 2004) showed pathological underweight in a small number of female students who explained their food restriction as driven by religious concerns.

A recent study in Fiji (Becker *et al.* 2002), reported in the *British Journal of Psychiatry*, sheds some light on current cultural contributions to eating disorders. Fiji's agricultural economy was undergoing a transition to an industrial one, which brought many changes, including the introduction of television in 1995. In Fiji, traditionally, a rounder body shape had been expected of females, so even in 1995 dieting was practically non-existent. After three years of television, including

American and British dramas, comedies, and advertising, things had changed. Sixty-nine percent of the study subjects (63 young women) reported dieting to lose weight, and 74 percent reported feeling too big or too fat. While there had been no reports of self-induced vomiting in 1995, 12 percent of the subjects reported this behaviour three years later. In their interviews the young women said things such as: they did not want to be "fat" like their mothers; they felt fatter when watching television shows; and they wanted to have the body shapes and lifestyles of the young women they saw on television.

The economic transition loosened the connection between children's lives and the values of the traditional culture of their parents, while television and advertising provided a different set of cultural values and ideals consistent with the new economy. In particular, the new economy created a paradigm shift regarding women's roles, creating attractive new opportunities for women that, through media and advertising, were associated with a slim female body. This combination of a culture in transition that has a particular effect on changing roles for women, and a positive meaning associated with thinness or avoidance of fat, is a potent contributor to the development of eating disorders (Nasser, Katzman and Gordon 2001).

In Gull and Lasegue's time, similar conditions contributed to increased risk of eating disorders. It was a time of economic transition from farming to industrialization, which created a burgeoning middle class in which food was plentiful. At the time, there were new opportunities opening up for families through their daughters. It had become possible for young women to marry higher up the social scale. If successful, they would increase the social status of their entire family. To be eligible, however, they had to make themselves appear "ladylike," so as to be attractive to men of higher economic class. To be seen as ladylike, girls and women learned they should maintain a petite and delicate appearance. They learned that through their food choices they could demonstrate virtue and spiritual purity – by eating no chocolate or sweets, which were considered too exciting, and by eating no meat, which was considered too strong for delicate ladies. For the first time in European countries daughters, not just sons, were seen as economically valuable. Girls would have felt considerable pressure to help their families by catching the attention of a man of means (Brumberg 1988).

Starting in the early 1930s the Great Depression, followed by the Second World War, created conditions unfavorable to eating disorders. Food shortages and threats to survival caused a temporary reversal in the valuation of body size. A 1933 ad in the American magazine *The Delineator* advertised a yeast-fortified beer to help women gain weight and featured a curvy woman telling a thinner woman "There's no need to be skinny now" (Figure 2.4).

Figure 2.4: Advertising weight gain
Reprinted from The Delineator *magazine, originally published by Butterick Publishing Company, March 1933. Currently The McCall Pattern Company. Reprinted with permission of The McCall Pattern Company*

However, by the early 1950s lower body weight had developed a cultural presence again – it was seen as an important way of gauging not just beauty, but also health and character, even though these associations do not stand up to reason. Through the 1960s and 1970s, women's roles were changing. Feminism challenged gender stereotypes and opened new opportunities for women. At the same time the economy shifted and technological and communication advances like television created the possibility of mass audiences for media messages about ideal body shape and size.

Several elements of present-day Western culture create a breeding ground for eating disorders. There is a kind of fat phobia that goes far beyond concern for the health of people who are above average weight (Boachie and Jasper 2006). Fat is an essential nutrient, but one might think it was inherently evil, judging by the reactions of the media and the conversations that occur almost everywhere. Being thin and "toned" is the dominant beauty ideal for women, while a more muscular ideal is dominant for men. Neither of these ideals allows for much in the way of fat, but there is a particular disadvantage for girls in this. Prior to puberty, boys and girls have about the same percentage of body fat. At puberty girls, who are developing and whose bodies are getting ready for menstruation, will have an increase in body fat. Boys at puberty will naturally lose fat and increase muscle. So while the muscular ideal for boys is consistent with the direction of their normal body development, the thin, toned ideal for girls is directly contrary to theirs.

Women's bodies are objectified and sexualized, which is to say they are treated as objects that exist for the pleasure or use of others. This happens through representations in the media and interpersonally, when women are looked at or "checked out," or given scores as they walk down the hall at school. Think of the Beach Volleyball rule at the Olympics: female athletes are required to wear bikinis, while male athletes can wear loose short-sleeved shirts and shorts. Girls learn to expect that their looks will be evaluated. This increases both their anxiety about appearance and body-related shame, because it is impossible for most to attain the beauty ideal. Constantly practicing self-monitoring and looking at their bodies from the outside disconnects girls and women from their internal body signals and interferes with full involvement and enjoyment of activities. One eye is always on "How do I look?" (Slater and Tiggemann 2002).

Women are also socialized to take care of others and to take responsibility for relationships – so they try to tune in to what the other person wants or needs (Miller 1991). This distances them from their own needs as they try to accommodate to the other, opening a gap that can lead to poor self-care and serious self-denial.

Finally, our culture is also preoccupied with perfection and control. The way women are encouraged to enact this preoccupation is through perfecting appearance and controlling appetite (Brown and Jasper 1993). Men have traditionally enacted this preoccupation through accomplishments, though more recently there is pressure for men to attend to appearance and body shape as well.

It's no wonder that the majority of adolescent girls are dissatisfied with their bodies, and at any given time nearly half of them are trying to lose weight. While about 3 percent develop anorexia or bulimia, up to 15 percent have significant levels of disordered eating (Academy for Eating Disorders 2009; Piran 2005).

WHEN WOMEN STARTED SMOKING

In the early twentieth century very few women smoked cigarettes. The idea of a woman smoking was repugnant. Gradually smoking became more socially acceptable for women, cigarettes became more easily available to them, and advertisers actively associated qualities valued in women with smoking in their advertisements. Before long, women started smoking in numbers comparable to men. However, even in this changed environment, *not all women started to smoke*. To explain why some women smoked and others didn't in the pro-smoking environment requires consideration of individual factors, including biological ones, which made some women more vulnerable and others less so (Bulik 2004).

Risk factors: adverse social experiences theory

Socio-cultural risk factors are not distributed equally – some girls or women have to cope with more of these than others (Bordo 2004). Teasing by peers, especially teasing about body weight, has been associated with low body satisfaction, low self-esteem, high depressive symptoms, and thinking about and attempting suicide, *regardless of actual* weight (Eisenberg, Neumark-Sztainer and Story 2003). Similarly, sexual harassment and sexual abuse may increase shame about the body, and thereby increase risk.

Since those with eating disorders often describe themselves as having had adverse body-related experiences, Piran and Thompson (2008) hypothesized that there may be a direct correlation between the amount of exposure one has to such experiences and vulnerability to eating disorders. Considering that girls and women are exposed to a substantial load of gender-related prejudice and of body-related intrusions, Piran and Thompson designed a study to find out whether there could be a cumulative relationship between adverse social experiences and the development of disordered eating and weight preoccupation. They found that experiences related to violations of body ownership (child or adult sexual and physical harassment and abuse) and experiences of exposure to prejudicial treatment (weightism and sexism) were cumulatively associated with disordered eating patterns. This suggests that adverse social experiences represent a significant risk factor for the development of eating disorders.

Risk factors: biological

Given that effective treatment of anorexia nervosa has continued to be very difficult, professionals have postulated various theories about biological causes, hoping that finding such a cause would lead to effective treatment; for instance, an effective medication might be found. Since most people with eating disorders are also depressed and there are effective medications for depression, the possibility of a common biological pathway to anorexia and depression was recently investigated. Contrary to their hypothesis, the researchers found that neuro-hormonal activity differs in depression and anorexia nervosa (Connan *et al.* 2007). Future research may be directed to the specific contribution of corticotrophin-releasing hormone (CRH) to the severity of weight loss in anorexia.

When there is a family history of an eating disorder, the risk that a young person will develop an eating disorder increases. Currently there is international collaborative research investigating the genetic factors that may be involved. There are profound metabolic, neurochemical, and brain structure alterations found in those with active anorexia and bulimia nervosa. Some disturbances in these areas, which may involve modulation of appetite, mood, cognitive function, impulse control, energy metabolism, and autonomic and hormonal systems, appear to persist after recovery (Klump *et al.* 2009). Genetics researchers are investigating these areas for genes that are factors in the development of eating disorders, but there have been no long-term prospective studies to date. It is clear that there is no gene or gene mutation that is responsible for causing anorexia or bulimia. Many genes may be involved and it is likely that epigenetic phenomena[2] will affect the impact any gene may have on increasing an individual's risk for an eating disorder (Klump 2009). The genes and epigenetic phenomena that contribute to eating disorders are likely to be part of the normal variation that occurs in the general population. That certain environments can turn normally occurring variations into vulnerability factors for serious illnesses with increasing prevalence reinforces how problematic an environment can be, and how much socio-cultural factors can contribute to endangering large numbers of young women (Jasper 2007).

Risk factors: neuropsychological (for anorexia nervosa)

Neuropsychological research studies related to anorexia nervosa are making some progress toward understanding what some pre-illness risk factors for some individuals could be. One study showed that subjects who tended to focus on fine details at the expense of the bigger picture had a higher frequency of body checking than those who did not (Agrawal and Lask 2009). This is known as "weak central coherence" and appears to be present during anorexia and after recovery from it. Other studies have been searching for a neuropsychological source of the inflexibility or rigidity seen in the behaviour of those with anorexia. This inflexibility is startling because it persists even when changing the behaviour would promote survival. Researchers are pursuing neural correlates for rigidity or difficulties with both

---

2   Non-genetic factors, like the presence or absence of a hormone, or the biological effects of psychological trauma, can cause genes to be expressed differently.

cognitive and behavioural shifts (Zastrow *et al.* 2009; Roberts *et al.* 2007). Emotion recognition and processing has also become a focus of study. Several studies have supported the idea that those with anorexia have difficulty identifying and labeling emotions (Oldershaw *et al.* 2011). Finally, some researchers have suggested that all of these features of anorexia may be explained by a disconnection between several brain structures, possibly manifested as a dysfunction of the insula, which is the area where various neural networks converge (Nunn *et al.* 2008).

A PROBLEM AT GRAND CENTRAL STATION

Most of the trains serving New York City from outlying areas converge at Grand Central Station. They bring people into the station in the mornings so they can work in New York City, and take them back to their home locations in the evening. If, on a particular day, nearly everyone who uses the trains were to be late arriving home from work, it would be a good idea to check whether the source of the problem was at Grand Central Station.

Similarly, it may be that a dysfunction in the insula, the brain structure where various neural networks converge, is responsible for several characteristic difficulties we see in those with anorexia, and may increase vulnerability to anorexia in those who do not yet have the illness.

There is no single factor that can be identified as the cause of an eating disorder. However, we can hypothesize something about vulnerability to eating disorders from understanding the role of individual vulnerabilities in the context of our culture.

LEARNING LANGUAGE

As human beings, we have all inherited the capacity to use language. This is a genetically based capacity. The specific language you speak will depend on the environment in which you learn. Depending on the language you speak, certain sounds will come easily to you, but will be more difficult for non-speakers of the language (e.g. rolling r's). The structure of your mouth and tongue will make it easier or harder for you to make the sounds required by your language. This is one type of interaction between genes and environment.

Risk factors: individual and psychological

It has been speculated that a particular temperament or characteristics can make girls more vulnerable to the spectrum of eating disorders. For example, being highly sensitive, detail-oriented, usually very intelligent, perfectionist, very structured, and having exceptional focus are qualities likely to be associated with anorexia. A girl with similar characteristics but with a more spontaneous or impulsive side would be likely to be more vulnerable to bulimia nervosa.

THE HEART SURGEON AND THE EMERGENCY DOCTOR

If you were looking for a heart surgeon, you would do very well to find someone who is perfectionist, highly structured, and very focused. Or if you wanted to build a bridge or a software program, those would be helpful characteristics, too. You would want someone conscientious, someone who will do the right thing. Or if you were in need of an emergency doctor, you would do very well to find someone with similar characteristics, but who is stimulated by change.

The same characteristics that help make a great 35-year-old female cardiac surgeon or an emergency doctor make a 13-year-old girl very vulnerable to anorexia or bulimia.

Starting a few years earlier, consider a ten-year-old girl with this temperament. She is often highly prized by teachers and considered no trouble by her parents. She hears her parents and teachers tell her what they want and is pleased to give it to them. She does very well because of her attention to detail and her pleasure at getting things right. Usually, at puberty things change. Developmentally she and her peers become more attuned to one another and less devoted to what their parents want. In this context, there is no longer any easy answer to the question "What is the right thing to do?" She may be overwhelmed by the choices now in front of her: if she wears make-up and tight clothes, she will fit in with peers, but may attract attention she doesn't know what to do with. If she smokes cigarettes, drinks or uses drugs, she will have an instant social group, but at the same time make herself too anxious to enjoy the effects and risk displeasing her parents.

DYNAMITE

A temperament may be like dynamite. Dynamite can be used to build roads through mountain areas or to put on a brilliant show of fireworks. But it can also be used to make landmines that blow up and destroy human bodies and lives. (See Figure 2.5.)

Figure 2.5: Dynamite
Drawing by Nadia Boachie 2010

This girl's temperament and intelligence create an awareness she's not yet emotionally mature enough to handle. In relating to others, she is excruciatingly aware of small changes in their facial expressions, voice tone, and body language. She will feel overwhelmed and very anxious not knowing what to respond to. Again, she will be looking for a way to simplify things, a clear way of choosing what to do. Suppose she reaches puberty slightly ahead of her peers and is subjected to body-related bullying: a group of boys or girls on Facebook comments on how fat she looks in a photo. Or suppose a grandparent dies and this girl's mother becomes inconsolable. The girl may then begin to feel ugly and/or out of control. Going on a diet and losing weight can provide her with an immediate and direct way of knowing whether she's done the right thing every day: eating less and losing weight is good, eating more or not losing weight is bad. To make this even more seductive, losing weight brings admiration from adults and peers alike. In this context perfectionism, being detail-oriented and highly structured, will facilitate the continued focus on dieting and weight control almost indefinitely, taking her beyond admiration and into the territory of disorder. Instead of her unique and autonomous voice beginning its development at this time, the authoritarian voice of an eating disorder takes over – bringing its deathly certainty about the right thing to do.

Other risk factors

Medical conditions that bring increased attention to food intake and the body, like diabetes, also increase risk, as do activities that require limiting body size, weight, or shape, like ballet dancing, gymnastics, and wrestling.

Young people who are uncomfortable discussing their problems with their parents will have additional stress. Teens from immigrant families who are acculturating to Western values may experience a split between family values and peer values. This can increase the difficulties involved in the transition from childhood to adolescence and simultaneously make it more difficult to discuss related problems with parents (Lock *et al.* 2001, p.4).

Finally, some research has shown that a maternal preoccupation with dietary restriction may also be a risk factor (Francis and Birch 2005). This may be related to the larger role that mothers have had in raising children, making their preoccupations more salient, or to the fact that women have been under pressure to diet far longer than have men, or to the fact that the researchers did not ask about fathers' eating habits. In any case, dietary restriction at home is a strong influence on children and may be a risk factor for eating disorders.

Risk factors: what about boys?

While boys tend to be protected from many of the cultural risk factors for girls, there is more pressure today on boys to pay attention to their appearance and to have an ideal body shape than there was 20 years ago. While being muscular is consistent with the normal development of boys, the standard of muscularity has intensified. Vulnerable young men may reduce their fat and carbohydrate intake in order to maximize muscle development, simultaneously increasing their vulnerability to eating disorders. While there is an increased risk for males who are gay due to the high value placed on appearance and body shape in gay culture, it is important not to assume that a boy with an eating disorder is gay. Heterosexual males do develop eating disorders too (Herrin and Matsumoto 2007).

Individual risk factors include a temperament similar to that described above. Other individual risk factors include having a higher-than-average body weight, experiencing teasing about body size, being later to reach puberty, participation in high-risk sports that favor thinness or have weight categories (wrestling, boxing, rowing, jockeying, etc.), and depression (Herrin and Matsumoto 2007).

Why have parents been blamed?

Probably parents have been blamed for three reasons. One is that the cultural risk factors tend to be invisible or are not noticed, and the biological factors are not yet known. Another is that our understanding of parenting today is that it should produce a well-socialized, healthy, happy child, rather than just a child who grows into an adult with the skills needed to provide or care for a family (Harden 2005). As a result, children who don't fit this picture, either because of temperament or because they have a mental health problem, tend to be seen as the result of poor or inadequate parenting. Mental health problems are poorly understood, often not recognized early, and carry stigma not associated with physical health problems. In one study, parents of children with mental illnesses reported that they had to drive the search for a diagnosis and push past professionals telling them that their child was just going through adolescence. Once the illness was identified, parents felt that the professionals held them responsible for the problem: their parenting skills were assessed or they were investigated for abuse (Harden 2005). The third reason is that looking after eating is considered to be a parental responsibility, so when parents do not realize that an eating disorder is an illness, they tend to blame themselves.

Parentectomy required?

Gull and Lasegue did not speculate on the cause of anorexia nervosa, except to suggest that an "emotional trauma" or "morbid mental state" preceded the illness (Bell 1985, pp.6–7). Both suggested that the patient's parents were somehow responsible for the illness, but did not delve deeply into this suggestion. They very clearly maintained, however, that it was essential to the patient's recovery that she be separated from her parents and treated by a physician who could establish moral control over the patient (Bell 1985; Brumberg 1988). Their confidence in their own ability to treat the young person was matched by their doubt in the efficacy of the parents to help her. This orientation to treatment persisted until relatively recently. Today, family-based therapy is considered to be the treatment of choice for children and adolescents with anorexia. Because the illness has grave consequences and can persist in the form of attitudes and beliefs, even after the young person has started eating again and has gained weight, it is crucial to involve the parents early on and throughout the illness, as they are key to the child's full recovery.

Young people don't realize how important eating is, and parents often don't see that as parents they are in a unique position to help the young person conquer her fear of eating. It is an illness and it so happens that parents are the ones who can help. You don't need special training to be a mother or father. The job is incredibly important and there is no pay.

BEST QUALIFIED

Someone is accused of committing a heinous crime. A jury, composed of ordinary people from all walks of life, will determine the defendant's future. The jury members are not specialists and they are not paid a large sum of money, but they are the right people for the job. So it is with the parents of an eating-disordered child – they are the ones who are best qualified to help.

Lasegue observed that the family becomes pre-occupied with the child's illness and all conversation revolves around it (Bell 1985). We would say that the family reorganizes itself around the illness, but this reorganization is not coordinated, as it would be in an illness where there is a clear treatment protocol, for example, diabetes. With anorexia there is often confusion in the family about what should be done, which is exhausting and can lead to the illness becoming chronic.

FIGHTING AN UNCONVENTIONAL WAR

It is like fighting an unconventional war, like drugs or terrorism, as opposed to fighting a traditional war. You can't prepare enough, you can never stop preparing, and it is unpredictable. There is constant and consistent fear – even if things are going well, you can't trust that they will continue to go well.

Understanding that eating disorders are illnesses and that the family has an essential role in the child's recovery enables family members to coordinate their efforts and to work consistently with one another against the eating disorder. Full recovery requires collaboration and concerted effort among parents, doctors, and other health professionals, school personnel, relatives, and friends.

Chapter 3

Recognizing and Diagnosing an Eating Disorder

Once an eating disorder has been diagnosed, it seems that it was obvious. However, there are many factors that contribute to making recognition and diagnosis of an eating disorder difficult.

CASE EXAMPLE: ANGELA

A mother has brought her daughter, Angela, to see their family physician. Angela is 12 years old and her mom says she has been complaining of abdominal pain. Angela had the flu a few weeks ago and threw up one or two times. Now she refuses to have her breakfast, saying that the milk makes her nauseous. Neither will she eat beef, which she finds "too chewy." Her mom says that Angela's sleep is poor: she doesn't fall asleep easily and she is tired when she wakes up. A teacher says that she seems preoccupied and does not pay attention at school. Her parents have noticed that Angela is losing weight.

Obstacles to recognition and diagnosis

In a busy clinic, there are many pressures on the family physician or general practitioner that work against taking the time required for a careful history and accurate diagnosis, even for those who have had adequate training in recognizing eating disorders. It is most likely that the family physician will refer Angela to a pediatrician, dietician, or child psychiatrist. According to a British study, only 2 percent of general practitioners and 33 percent of pediatricians accurately diagnose eating disorders (Bryant-Waugh *et al.* 1992). Parents may take their child to the doctor many times before the eating disorder is recognized. This is not the fault of physicians. Eating disorders are relatively rare and medical students and residents usually get very little training that would help in recognizing them. But for the parents of a child with an eating disorder, it's the most important thing in the world, and therefore they are the ones most likely to recognize the eating disorder in children and teens (Lask *et al.* 2005).

Although it is always difficult to know when an eating disorder started, this is not unusual with medical illnesses in general. For example, with hypertension, a person doesn't notice anything going wrong with his circulatory system. He may go to the doctor after getting headaches. It's similar with the flu.

THE FLU

With the flu, you get the bug before you know you have it. You may be sneezing a little more than usual, and not realize that you are spreading it around. By the time you have a diagnosis, other people around you have already caught it. This is why we look for an immunization.

On the other hand, neither the person with flu, nor the person with hypertension will try to conceal the fact that they have symptoms. But young people developing eating disorders will. Parents may have suspicions, but even young children will conceal the disorder from family and friends (Bryant-Waugh *et al.* 1992). There may be a teacher or friend at school, where the child or teen is not as diligent about hiding things, who notices that something is wrong. Still, this does not translate into a diagnosis. Usually a sign or symptom will have gone on for quite a while before an eating disorder is diagnosed. Many of the symptoms are not specific to eating disorders, which contributes to the difficulty in recognizing them. Family physicians may not know interview techniques that could prompt disclosure of eating disorder thoughts and behaviours (DeSocio *et al.* 2006). Many parents and doctors may be unaware that the disorder can occur in young children between the ages of seven and eleven (Bryant-Waugh *et al.* 1992). It is very important also, to be aware that several specific characteristics may interfere with timely diagnosis in children and adolescents. One is that young girls may not have reached menarche and therefore cannot "miss" a period, something that would alert the parent of an older girl that something is wrong.[3] Second is that healthy children and young teens are in the process of growing in height, which requires ongoing increases in weight. However, weight gain at this time may be interpreted by the child as "getting fat," rather than as part of normal growth, and she may diet in order to remedy what she sees as a fault (Bryant-Waugh *et al.* 1992). When a child is merely maintaining her weight or is losing even a small amount of weight, she will not grow taller; therefore weight maintenance or loss should be read as a signal that something is wrong (Bryant-Waugh *et al.* 1992).

SENDING A ROCKET TO THE MOON

If you want to send a rocket to the moon, you have to take into account that the moon is a moving target. You have to estimate where the moon will be when the rocket reaches it. If you aim the rocket toward the place where the moon is now, then by the time the rocket gets there, the moon will have moved away. (See also Figure 4.5 on p.88.)

Similarly, when estimating the weight a young person should be in six months' time, you have to take into account how tall she is expected to be, and shoot toward a weight that will support increased height.

Trickiness of eating disorders

When a teen is depressed there may be sleep troubles, anger and irritability, frequent crying, withdrawal from some friends and family, as well as other signs and symptoms. Though there may be initial difficulty communicating with the teen about her depression, both parent and teen will agree that there is a problem and share

---

3   Clearly this is also a factor in the diagnosis of boys with eating disorders.

the goal of finding a way to resolve the depression. With an eating disorder, the very signs and symptoms that indicate to doctors and parents that *there is a problem*, for example weight loss, indicate to the teen that she is successfully *solving* her "problem." Someone may recently have praised her for losing weight, so when she feels the boniness of her hips and is told by the doctor that her heart rate is low, she feels reassured that she is doing the right thing. Just as parents and doctors start worrying and calling it an illness, she is feeling elated at her achievement.

Many children and teens with eating disorders are very smart and have been trusted by their parents because, prior to the eating disorder, their behaviour has not been cause for worry. Being very smart makes a child appear mature, but in fact does not enable her to manage emotions better than any other child (Bainbridge 2009). However, it is more difficult to notice such a child's emotions. An eating disorder may even help her to hide her intense emotions and her sensitivity in relationships. When a mother feels concerned about the fact that her daughter is always cold, the daughter may say that there is nothing to worry about and her mother may then put her worries to rest, not realizing that her daughter has answered "no," not because she is actually alright, but because she does not want mom to worry. If her mom worries, the daughter will feel guilty, or perhaps she will feel she is losing the control she perceived to be the reason why people trusted her in the first place.

The initial signs and symptoms of eating disorders are so variable that they are difficult to read and can create a picture that is consistent with other illnesses. For instance, if a mother takes her daughter to the doctor because she is always cold and the daughter goes for a run just before the appointment, the doctor will find that she is not cold and will disagree with mom that there is something wrong. Or, if the mom thinks, "My child is depressed," and takes her to see a psychiatrist, the daughter may not be seen as having a typical depression and the doctor may tell the mom that she needn't worry. All of these visits take time, and during this time the eating disorder gets entrenched. For example, the flow chart in Figure 3.1 demonstrates some ways that delay in recognition and diagnosis may happen.

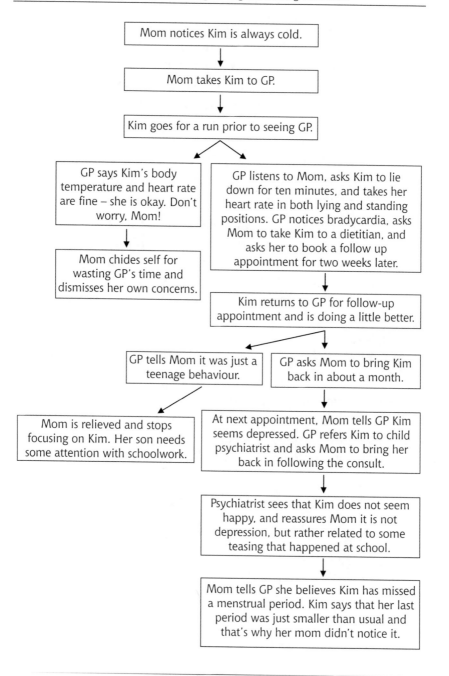

Figure 3.1: Flowchart – delay in recognizing and diagnosing an eating disorder

Delays like those in the flow chart can continue indefinitely without it being anyone's fault. Eating disorders are not generally well understood and they are illnesses that thrive on "splitting": that is, disruptions in relationships between parents or between parents and health professionals occur due to the young person's misguided trust in the eating disorder. Such disruptions are "opportunities" for the eating disorder to gain more ground and eating disorders are illnesses of opportunity. General practitioners who use a relational approach with their patients can help prevent eating disorders or diagnose them early. As Siridopoulos (2007) observes:

> Allowing the patient more opportunities for in-depth and intimate discussions on issues such as body image and self-esteem, with a more comprehensive focus would be ideal... using part of a check-up visit to inquire about school, family, nutrition, and extracurricular activities can identify that problems are developing or provide an outlet for adolescents to discuss problems. Discussions with the adolescent alone and the parents alone could provide insight into the home and school environment. (Siridopoulos 2007, p.23)

The idea is that children and teens need an unhurried environment and a relationship with their doctor that encourages them to talk about what is happening with them. Even one missed period or an episode of vomiting reported to the doctor should be taken seriously.

THE DAY THE LEVEES BROKE

Before hurricane Katrina, we knew the levees in New Orleans were in need of strengthening. They needed to be thicker and higher. A delay in doing something about this problem resulted in immense flooding when a huge hurricane overwhelmed them.

Family doctors should ask lots of questions. For example, if a girl loses one period or reports vomiting, this should be taken seriously and investigated. With an eating disorder, waiting too long can have very serious consequences, including impaired growth, osteoporosis, heart problems, and even death.

It is always preferred that an illness be prevented; however, over the years, preventing eating disorders has proved to be very difficult. Once an eating disorder has developed, early diagnosis and treatment give the best chance for a good outcome (Weiner 1999), but there are several factors that have been seen to delay diagnosis:

- The illness usually starts with psychological changes, which are not easy to discern.

- The first visible evidence of the illness tends to be a medical complication, like bradycardia (slow heart rate), postural hypotension (low blood pressure), visible weight loss, or fainting episodes.

- The young person often denies there is a problem.

Who is qualified to make the diagnosis?

At a glance, you would think a psychiatrist, or in some cases a psychologist, would make the diagnosis first. Both of the main sources used for making the diagnosis of an eating disorder, the ICD-10 and the DSM-IV-TR, are for psychiatric diagnoses. (See Appendix I for a full listing of the diagnostic categories.) Unlike other psychiatric illnesses, however, the way an eating disorder usually gets identified is through its medical complications. Family doctors may identify the problem as a serious one only after there are clear medical complications and then send the child to a pediatrician, who may be able to see the eating disorder through these complications. At this stage a psychiatrist might be consulted to confirm the diagnosis. Parents often say that, once they realized there was something wrong, they had to persist in seeking help for their child, and that not until the child had deteriorated even more did they get an accurate diagnosis. It may be that the best route to early diagnosis would be for parents to have direct access to specialist consultation for a suspected eating disorder, for example a pediatrician, psychiatrist, or psychologist.

It is usually seven to thirteen years before a teen herself will seek treatment for an eating disorder and then, on average, it takes five to seven years for recovery. If she is 14 when first diagnosed, then without parental intervention she could be 21 or older when she enters treatment, and 26 or more by the time she recovers.

When parents have a real appreciation for the effects of an eating disorder on their child, they can help her accept treatment by taking the decision for them. On the other hand, parents without such an appreciation may instead think they are helping their child by advocating for her to "have another chance" to deal with the eating disorder on her own. This provides the eating disorder with more opportunity to grow. A full appreciation can help parents take action on behalf of their child sooner rather than later.

A diagnosis

CASE EXAMPLE: ANGELA

Looking back at the example introduced at the beginning of this chapter, a thorough examination by a family physician or pediatrician would include the following. When parents are worried, as Angela's mother is, then take the time for a thorough history and do a full physical exam to rule out physical illness. Effective history taking will mean asking questions, both of parent and child together, and individually. Appropriate questions will include:

- whether the "flu" Angela had may have been the result of, for example, a streptococcal infection

- their impressions of when the abdominal pain started (considering the possibility that physical symptoms such as abdominal pain may be related to teasing or bullying, or to hunger due to dieting)

- when they noticed that Angela stopped eating breakfast

- why Angela has stopped eating breakfast, what she eats at lunchtime and at supper, and when she started to find that beef is "too chewy"

- if Angela is involved in any sports or if she plays games at school: "What do you like to do after school?" (assessing physical activity level and any recent changes in this level)

- why Angela thinks her teacher says she seems preoccupied and not paying attention the way she did before (assessing emotional state/ possible bullying or social problems at school, possible effects of dieting)

- what Angela is thinking about when she tries to go to sleep

- asking her if she is worried about any of the changes she has noticed in her body (saying that Angela's body will be changing as she grows and goes through puberty – focusing on normal body changes in size and shape, rather than weight, allows the adolescent to express concerns with body image and to ask questions).

Although Angela has a recent history of vomiting, this appears to be limited to the time when she had the "flu." Since she is only 12 and bulimia nervosa is unusual in young children, it is probable that she does not have bulimia nervosa. If her answers to questions about body changes give evidence of body image distortion or preoccupation with weight and shape, then Angela is likely developing anorexia nervosa. Pediatric Autoimmune Neuropsychiatric Disorders Associated with Streptococcal Infections (PANDAS) (see Appendix I) is very rare, but checking whether she could have had a streptococcal infection will help determine whether her anorexia nervosa could be PANDAS-related. If Angela does not express any weight or shape preoccupation, then the combination of weight loss, determined food refusal, and evidence of anxiety or depression suggest that a diagnosis of Food Avoidance Emotional Disorder (FAED) would be accurate.

Signs and symptoms of eating disorders

Eating disorders are systemic illnesses that affect the whole body and have both physical and psychological effects, as illustrated in Figures 3.2 and 3.3.

Table 3.1 lists some of the more common signs and symptoms. Many of the symptoms are the direct result of starvation and/or abnormal eating behaviours. Even though it may not be obvious that bulimia is a starving illness, because many of those who have it are not underweight, the bingeing that is characteristic of it is caused by food restriction to begin with.

In spite of these signs and symptoms, parents and the child or teen herself may think she is not seriously ill, because she is still doing well in school.

ELECTRICAL BLACKOUT AND PARLIAMENT

Q: If there is an electrical blackout and there is only one back-up generator to provide energy, where do you think the energy will be shunted to: Parliament Hill/the White House, or our homes?

A: To Parliament Hill/the White House, of course.

The body will always shunt limited available energy to the brain rather than any other organ, including the heart, in order that executive decisions can be made. The skin, which is a huge consumer of energy and makes a less significant contribution to survival, can be given less to work with. Similarly, the organs of procreation are shut down because energy can't be put into future generations when the survival of the current generation is in question. The brain will be protected more than any other organ.

Table 3.1: Signs and symptoms of anorexia nervosa and bulimia nervosa

Anorexia nervosa		Bulimia nervosa	
Symptoms	*Signs*	*Symptoms*	*Signs*
Weight loss	Emaciation (loss of subcutaneous fat tissue)	Irregular menses	Calluses on the back of the hand
Amenorrhea		Esophageal burning	
Irritability	Hyperactivity	Non-focal abdominal pain	Salivary gland hypertrophy
Sleep disturbances	Bradycardia	Lethargy	Erosion of dental enamel
Fatigue	Hypotension		
Weakness	Dry skin	Fatigue	Periodontal disease
Headache	Brittle hair/nails	Headache	
Dizziness	Hair loss on scalp	Constipation/diarrhea	Dental caries
Faintness	"Yellow" skin, especially palms		Petechiae
Constipation		Swelling of hands/feet	Perioral irritation
Non-focal abdominal pain	Lanugo hair		Mouth ulcers
	Cyanotic (blue) and cold hands and feet	Frequent sore throats	Hermatemesis
Feeling of "fullness"	Edema (ankle, periorbital)	Depression	Edema (ankle, periorbital)
Polyuria		Swollen cheeks	
Intolerance of cold			Abdominal bloating

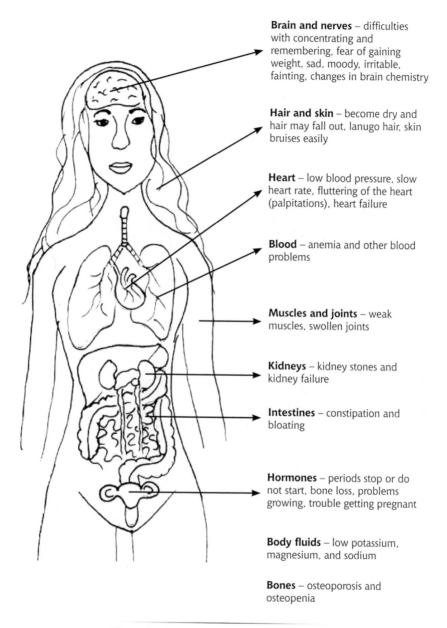

Brain and nerves – difficulties with concentrating and remembering, fear of gaining weight, sad, moody, irritable, fainting, changes in brain chemistry

Hair and skin – become dry and hair may fall out, lanugo hair, skin bruises easily

Heart – low blood pressure, slow heart rate, fluttering of the heart (palpitations), heart failure

Blood – anemia and other blood problems

Muscles and joints – weak muscles, swollen joints

Kidneys – kidney stones and kidney failure

Intestines – constipation and bloating

Hormones – periods stop or do not start, bone loss, problems growing, trouble getting pregnant

Body fluids – low potassium, magnesium, and sodium

Bones – osteoporosis and osteopenia

Figure 3.2: How anorexia affects your body
Adapted from the National Women's Health Information Centre website by Zaleekah Boachie 2010

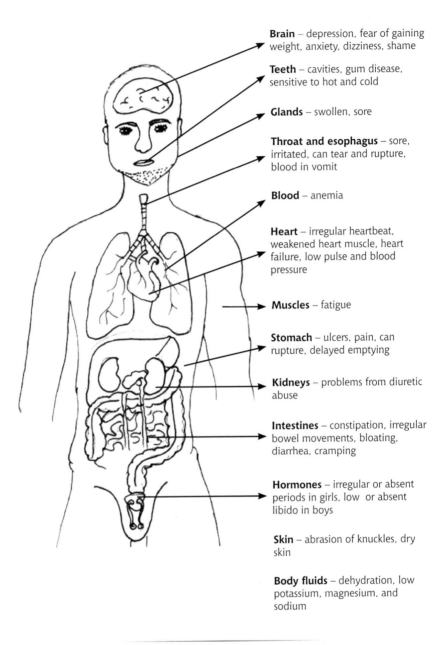

Brain – depression, fear of gaining weight, anxiety, dizziness, shame

Teeth – cavities, gum disease, sensitive to hot and cold

Glands – swollen, sore

Throat and esophagus – sore, irritated, can tear and rupture, blood in vomit

Blood – anemia

Heart – irregular heartbeat, weakened heart muscle, heart failure, low pulse and blood pressure

Muscles – fatigue

Stomach – ulcers, pain, can rupture, delayed emptying

Kidneys – problems from diuretic abuse

Intestines – constipation, irregular bowel movements, bloating, diarrhea, cramping

Hormones – irregular or absent periods in girls, low or absent libido in boys

Skin – abrasion of knuckles, dry skin

Body fluids – dehydration, low potassium, magnesium, and sodium

Figure 3.3: How bulimia affects your body
*Adapted from the National Women's Health Information
Centre website by Zaleekhah Boachie 2010*

Subtle signs and symptoms

Parents often observe more subtle changes, like the following. It is important that even after a young person has recovered from an eating disorder, parents continue to watch for these. This is a secretive illness and parents need a mindset where alarms will ring when these changes occur:

- Often wears baggy or loose-fitting clothing, either to hide weight loss or because of a profound sense of body dissatisfaction.

- Wearing warm clothes that seem too warm or heavy for the conditions.

- Rarely observed to eat with anyone: "I ate before I got here."

- Increased use of caffeinated drinks (coffee/cola), smoking, and gum chewing.

- Recent adoption of a vegetarian diet (regardless of rationale).

- Preoccupation with food: loves to cook for others, but won't join in the prepared meal; zealously collects recipes and cookbooks.

- Becomes very defensive or anxious when body, weight, or shape issues are openly discussed or challenged, even if not about self directly.

- Finds holidays and special occasions to be very stressful (celebrations usually revolve around large meals, constant eating, and drinking).

- Odd or bizarre eating habits or rituals: must cut food into certain size pieces, eats plate of food in a specific order, deconstructs food as prepared, takes an unusually long time to finish meal.

- Won't participate in activities where one's body can be scrutinized (swimming, sunbathing; won't use public showers at fitness centre).

- Unusual physical activity, such as taking the dog for a walk even in bad weather.

THE STEALTH BOMBER

Stealth aircraft use technology that makes them very difficult to detect, even by radar. Their attack missions cannot be prevented by conventional means. If you are looking for a stealth bomber with binoculars, you will think, "Nothing is there." In the meantime, it will have dropped bombs and disappeared before you realize it has hit you.

Mom: Sweetie, are you eating enough?

Daughter: Yes, Mom, I ate a lot over at my friend's house.

An eating disorder is like a stealth bomber: very challenging to detect and very destructive. Most of the typical questions we ask to uncover it are about as effective as using binoculars to look for the bomber.

Medical complications

Again, because eating disorders are systemic illnesses, there are many complications. Those that are most likely connected with mortality are described below. Young people take us more seriously when we discuss these complications. It helps them consider making changes. Starvation is associated with low blood pressure and bradycardia (low heart rate). Weight loss has been associated with the development of mitral valve prolapse. Fluid and electrolyte imbalances (hypokalemia or low potassium, most commonly), brought on by dehydration due to repeated purging or restriction of fluids, can result in conduction abnormalities. Life-threatening arrhythmias may also occur, resulting, for instance, from prolonged QTc interval (Levy and Curfman 2006).

1. Bradycardia or low heart rate

THE TELEVISION REMOTE CONTROL

A good heart rate, or normal sinus rhythm, is 60–100 beats per minute. In this case the heart's natural pacemaker, the SA node, will be working well. It is like having a functioning remote control for the television.

When the heart rate slows down to between 40 and 60, the AV junction takes over – the SA node can't do it on its own. This is like having to use the controls on the front of the television to change channels and volume.

When the heart rate drops below 40, the heart may not be pumping enough blood to meet the body's needs. Ventricles will be firing on their own. This is like having to open up the television and fiddle directly with the wires inside in order to get the channels to change.

As the heart rate slows down due to lack of nutrition, the control of its rate shifts from the sinus node, to the AV junction, to the ventricles (see Figure 3.4).

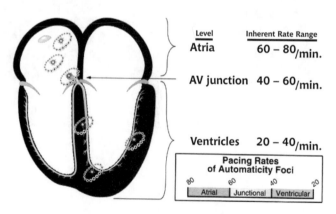

The automaticity foci of each "level" (the atria, the AV junction, and the ventricles are each a "level") have a general range of pacemaking rate. Although all foci of a given level pace within a general rate range, each individual automaticity focus has its own precise *inherent rate* at which it paces.

Figure 3.4: Automaticity foci
Reprinted from Dubin 2000 with permission from Dale Dubin, MD

Figure 3.5 shows a chest X-ray in which the patient's small heart is barely visible – it had shrunk in size due to her weight loss and purging.

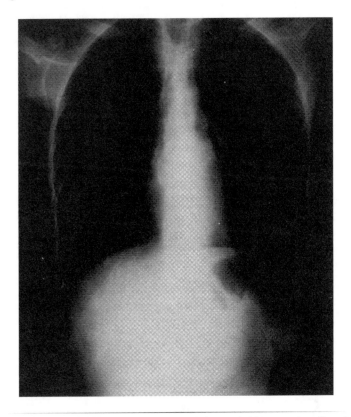

Figure 3.5: X-ray of heart elongated and thinned due to eating disorder
Reprinted from Andersen 1999 with permission of the Johns Hopkins University Press

2. Postural hypotension or low blood pressure once bradycardia has developed

THE HALF-FULL BOTTLE

Get a bottle and fill it full. Get another bottle and fill it halfway. The full one is full whether it is standing up or lying down. If the half-full one is standing up, you have to use something like a straw to get the liquid to the top. If the bottle is lying on its side, the liquid will easily reach the mouth of the bottle with no special effort or technology.

When a person lies flat, their blood pressure becomes lower because it takes minimal effort to pump blood from one area of the body to another. If the person suddenly gets up, then because of gravity the heart has to work twice as hard to pump the blood to get it from the lower part of the body to the upper parts. This is one reason why exercise is not recommended for those with eating disorders.

Figure 3.6: Half-full bottle
Drawing by Nadia Boachie 2011

3. Torsades arrhythmia
(associated with high mortality)

Torsades is a fast-paced arrhythmia of the heart that is associated with high mortality. Persistent purging and low weight can cause hypokalemia (too little potassium). In the context of prolonged QTc interval of the heart, this will cause about 10 percent of patients to die.

THE FLUORESCENT LIGHT AND THE INCANDESCENT LIGHT

A fluorescent light flickers for quite a while before the bulb finally burns out, but an incandescent light goes out without any warning. Use the switch on a light to see this.

A teen who continues with purging behaviour is at risk of developing a heart problem that may kill her without warning.

DRIVING WITH NO GAS

Imagine a young person is driving her parents' car from Florida to New York and has filled the gas tank for the trip. Somewhere along the way, she notices the red light showing that she should fill up soon. Usually an adult would stop at the very next gas station, but a teen enjoying the music with her friends may think she can make it to the next city, and will just keep driving. When the car stops suddenly, she will be surprised.

Usually the teens who develop eating disorders are less risk-taking than average. They start off as girls who tend not to challenge authority, but the eating disorder gives them a willingness to risk and to be "in your face." They may underestimate the danger they are in and can crash suddenly.

4. Osteoporosis

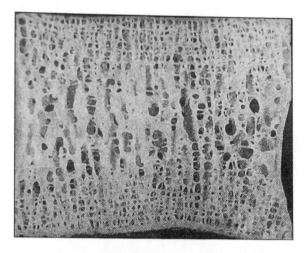

a) Healthy bone tissue

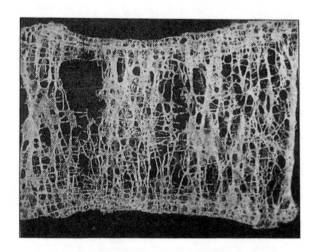

b) Osteoporosis due to eating disorder

Figure 3.7: Normal bone density compared to osteoporosis
Reprinted from Morris 2001 with permission of the editor

OSTEOPOROSIS AND THE BRICK WALL

Severe loss of bone density, or osteoporosis, is like having bricks or stones built up to make a wall, but with no cement holding them together. The wind can easily blow them down.

Bone density is built up more during adolescence than at any other period of development. Once a young woman has reached the end of her teen years, her bone density begins to decrease very slowly. An eating disorder can interfere with the building up of bone density, causing osteopenia or osteoporosis, usually conditions found in elderly women. Figure 3.7a shows healthy bones, and Figure 3.7b shows bones affected by osteoporosis due to an eating disorder.

5. Effects on the brain

Research has shown that the brain loses white and gray matter through starvation (Katzman *et al.* 1996; Chui *et al.* 2008). Those with anorexia nervosa showed larger cerebro-spinal fluid (CSF) volumes and deficits in cortical gray and white brain matter compared to controls (see Figure 3.8). The degree of larger CSF volumes is related to the degree of starvation. Those who had irregular or no menses showed significant cognitive deficits.

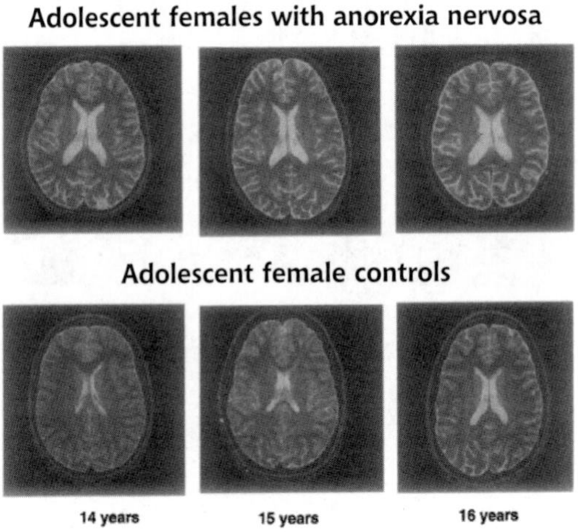

Figure 3.8: MRI in adolescents with anorexia nervosa vs. controls
Reprinted from Katzman et al. 1996 with permission from Elsevier

6. Re-feeding syndrome

There are also serious complications that can arise with re-feeding someone who is starving. Parents as well as doctors need to understand these.

THE FACTORY AND THE RECESSION

Imagine there is an economic recession and the need for cars is much reduced. The car factory only needs to produce ten cars per week. The plant cuts down on staff and supplies. Then suddenly an order comes in for 200 cars that are needed within two weeks. Trying to fill this order, the factory crashes, because it doesn't have enough resources to supply what is demanded.

It is the same for a child who has been starving and is suddenly re-fed a large amount of carbohydrates. Her system does not have sufficient resources to metabolize this food and will crash. When eager to re-feed a young person, we have to slow down to avoid causing heart failure. If the child/adolescent has lost 25 percent of their body weight, even if they are willing to eat, they should come into hospital.

Co-morbidities

It is very common for children and teens with eating disorders to have co-existing major depression, including suicidality; or to have anxiety disorders, including generalized anxiety disorder, social phobia, obsessive-compulsive disorder (OCD), and panic disorder. Substance use disorders are also relatively common, especially among those with bulimia nervosa, but psychosis is rare, occurring no more frequently than in the general population. Studies report varied incidence of mood disorders and and substance abuse. In adults with eating disorders, Blinder, Cumella and Sanathara (2006) found 94 percent to have mood disorders, most commonly depression, 56 percent to have anxiety disorders, and 22 percent to have substance use disorders. Young people understand these common co-morbid conditions relatively easily. Nevertheless, they are complicating factors that affect recovery, either by making it difficult to get to the core symptoms of the eating disorder, as in OCD, or because the eating disorder makes it difficult to treat the co-morbid condition, as in depression.

1. Depression

Depression may affect the person prior to the onset of the eating disorder, or can be an effect of starvation and the relational impact of the eating disorder. The latter type of depression may resolve with weight restoration and subsequent reconnection with friends and family, without the use of medication or specific psychological treatment. Pre-existing depression can be more difficult because with low weight, medication is less effective and cognitive processing is compromised. Some weight restoration is required before depression can be treated (Blinder *et al.* 2006).

2. Suicidality

There is little or no research on suicidality in children and adolescents with eating disorders. However, we know that about 10 percent of those with eating disorders who eventually die are suicides. In an adult study, those with anorexia tended to have a higher frequency of suicide attempts than those with bulimia. Previous studies have found suicidality to be more likely in the binge/purge subtype than in the restricting subtype of anorexia. One finding of interest is that among subjects with anorexia or bulimia, attempters and non-attempters differed on measures of personality characteristics and interpersonal relations, and not on measures of eating-related symptoms or attitudes. The results from this study suggest that particularly among bulimic women those who saw themselves as lacking in self-efficacy, who had more difficulty identifying internal states, and who were distrustful of others, were more likely to have made a suicide attempt. Among those with anorexia, those who saw themselves as lacking in self-efficacy were most likely to have made a suicide attempt (Favaro and Santonastaso 1997).

3. Anxiety disorders

An eating disorder can mask social phobia, panic disorder, and generalized anxiety. These co-existing conditions become more blatant when the young person's weight has been restored at least to some extent. Once cognitive processing has resumed more normally, cognitive behavioural therapy, including desensitization, along with medication such as a selective seretonin re-uptake inhibitor (SSRI), can be very helpful. Sometimes the degree of anxiety that exists about eating is so great that medication may be needed for the young person to tolerate eating and weight gain at all. The use of atypical anti-psychotics for these cases will be discussed in Chapter 7 (p.141).

OCD is very prevalent and works in partnership with the eating disorder. A child or teen who is fearful of contamination may be especially susceptible to fear of being fat and of eating fat, worrying about the healthfulness of "junk" foods, meat, and any food with fat content. Avoiding these foods can then become like avoiding other "contaminants." A program of exposure and response prevention or desensitization to these foods is a common part of eating disorder treatment. If these behaviours are not addressed, they will serve as a risk factor for relapse.

ENGLISH LITERACY TEST

Every high-school student in Ontario, Canada, must pass an English literacy test in order to qualify for university. Passing the test does not guarantee the student a place in a university, but without it the student cannot get in.

Prognosis

A prospective 15-year follow-up study of adolescents with anorexia showed that three-quarters of the 95 patients fully recovered. The course of recovery was protracted, with a median time of 72 months. Predictors of chronic outcome included early weight loss after hospital discharge, extreme compulsive drive to exercise at discharge, and a history of poor social relating preceding onset of the illness. Predictors of a longer recovery time were disturbances in family relationships and extreme compulsivity in daily routines (Strober et al. 1997).

Conclusion

The physical, psychological, and social effects of an eating disorder together cause a regression for the young person just at a time when there would usually be intense development. If the eating disorder is not treated early on, the impact of this regression is likely to be magnified, and this in turn will contribute to the illness becoming chronic. Clearly there is a need for further research in this field. However, it is certain that eating disorders are damaging to the development of children and adolescents and should not be left undiagnosed or untreated.

Chapter 4

Outpatient Management

The majority of eating disorders are managed on an outpatient basis. As discussed in Chapter 3, one of the main stumbling blocks to accessing treatment is having the eating disorder recognized and diagnosed. In Canada, once a family doctor suspects an eating disorder, the child or teen will be referred to medical colleagues for further investigation and diagnosis: a specialist eating disorder program, a psychiatrist, a psychologist, a community pediatrician, or the emergency department.

This chapter is concerned with what happens when a patient is referred to a specialist eating disorder program for assessment.

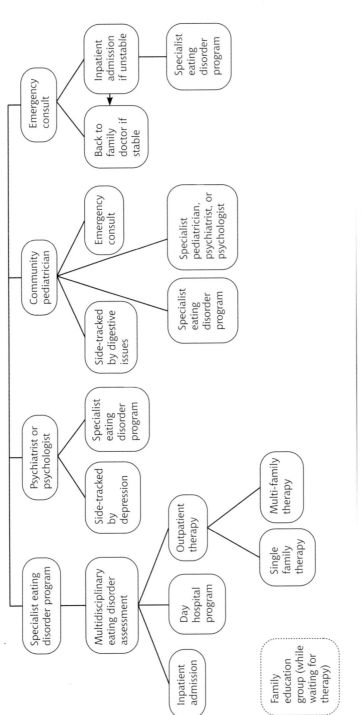

Figure 4.1: Family doctor refers after suspecting an eating disorder*
*This is an example from the Canadian health care system

Family doctor refers to a specialized eating disorders program for formal assessment[4]

CASE EXAMPLE: MOIRA

Moira's family doctor called to make a referral for her to a specialized eating disorders program. She had been seeing the 14-year-old for over six months. It had started with an apparent loss of appetite. Moira said she didn't feel like eating and she had lost some weight. Dr. Chau had checked but could not find any signs of a physical illness. She encouraged Moira to eat more and asked Moira's mom, Stephanie, to support her to do so.

At the next visit, Moira reported that her new friends in high school said she looked great and so she did not think she needed to eat more. Stephanie said that she could not get Moira to eat more. Dr. Chau sent Moira to a dietitian, thinking that it would help her accept more food if she heard a dietitian say it was necessary.

Stephanie brought her back a month later. Things were not getting better. Moira said she could not eat what the dietitian prescribed, because it was far too much and would make her feel ill to eat it all. Just before seeing Moira and her mom this time, Dr. Chau had looked at the calendar. It had been six months.[5] Dr. Chau chatted with them for a while before starting her examination. Stephanie said she suspected that Moira had not had a menstrual period for a few months. When Dr. Chau asked, Moira admitted this to be true, but was not worried about it. She said she liked not having the bother of periods.

Dr. Chau's concern increased as she took Moira's weight and height. Her weight was the same as at her last visit and her height had not increased even by a centimeter in half a year. Then Dr. Chau took Moira's blood pressure, first with Moira lying down – it was 80/40; then standing – it was 100/50. The difference between the two measures suggested Moira might be susceptible to feeling faint when making sudden changes in her posture, especially from lying down to standing, a condition usually referred to as "postural hypotension."[6] This would be a sign that Moira's heart was having difficulty pumping blood to her vital organs. The two measures should have been more like 100/65 and 100/70. A young person's heart should not have difficulty with the change from lying to standing. Moira's heart rate was also troubling to Dr. Chau. It was 45 when she was lying down and 75 when she stood up. Lying or standing, the

---

4   This is just one example of how a referral for an eating disorder assessment could go.

5   Weight loss and health deterioration can occur very rapidly, even over much shorter periods of time than six months and in these acute cases can be especially dangerous for health.

6   See "The half-full bottle" metaphor on p.61.

heart rate should not usually be less than 60, and the difference between the two should not be more than 20.

Dr. Chau concluded that Moira's condition had worsened considerably and she felt that Moira needed an assessment with a specialized eating disorders program. Moira said this was "stupid" and added, "There's nothing wrong with me. Remember, I just got 90 percent on my math test!" She glared at her mom. Dr. Chau was extremely relieved when Moira's mom said calmly, "Yes, honey, I do remember, but if your heart is in trouble, your brain will soon follow it there, and we are not going to stand by while that happens."

Dr. Chau placed a call to the eating disorders program intake worker. Then she prepared the required forms with detailed information about Moira's history as well as her signs and symptoms, to be faxed in by her secretary. Soon Moira's parents would get a phone call telling them where and when to bring Moira for a formal assessment for an eating disorder.

Intake worker screens the referral[7]

Teresa put down the phone after talking to Dr. Chau. She looked over the forms that came through by fax. She reviewed them carefully to see if there were any safety concerns including self-harm or suicidality, and medically severe bradycardia or low potassium levels, that might indicate a crisis response would be needed. There were none in Moira's case, so Teresa forwarded the forms to the pediatrician (in some cases this would be the psychiatrist) who headed the eating disorders assessment team.

Soon after, the paediatrician let Teresa know that although there was good reason to be concerned that Moira had an eating disorder, there were no acute medical issues nor any psychiatric co-morbidities – most commonly depression, anxiety, or OCD. For this reason, and also because Moira was not pre-pubertal, she would be placed on the waiting list for an assessment, rather than being prioritized for an immediate assessment. She would need to be monitored regularly while waiting, in case her vital signs were to deteriorate. It could take up to three months before the assessment would take place.

Assessment day

Moira, her 17-year-old brother, and her parents arrived for the eating disorders assessment. Moira was given questionnaires to fill out.[8] The secretary told the family the assessment plan. The team pediatrician (or nurse) would see

---

7   This is just one example of how an intake process could be organized.

8   These are standard questionnaires used to capture common co-morbidities like anxiety and depression.

Moira first for a medical examination.[9] Then the whole family would meet with the family therapist. Following this, Moira would meet individually with the psychiatrist, and then the dietitian. After these meetings the team members would meet with one another to review their findings, and finally the team would meet with the family to discuss their observations, make recommendations, and answer questions.[10]

At last it was time for Moira's family to meet with the team. The family therapist, Janine, introduced parents and brother to the dietitian and psychiatrist. She expressed appreciation for the family members' openness in the interviews, and said that the psychiatrist would explain the diagnosis, and then the team would make their treatment recommendations.

Dr. Achebe said, "Moira has the restricting form of anorexia nervosa. This is a very serious illness. It means that she is either not eating enough or finds other ways to get rid of food eaten, such that her body is not supported to be healthy and to grow. At her age it is crucial that she eats enough food, not just to maintain her health, but because it is essential to her growth."

He continued, "As adults our bodies may not need as much energy because our growth rate is much slower. Moira's body will not let her become taller because it can't afford to put any energy into growing in height while it is using every bit of energy it has to protect major internal organs such as her heart and her brain. That may be the reason why she has stopped menstruating. It is as if the body is saying, until it has enough energy for itself to continue surviving, it won't let any energy go into reproduction."

GENERATOR

If my child is so sick – her heart rate is low and so on – why is she so smart? She is still getting the highest marks in school.

If there is an electrical blackout and there's only one generator, where do you think the one generator will be shunted to: Parliament Hill or our homes? The body will always shunt the energy to the brain rather than the heart, in order that executive decisions can be made. (See also "Electrical blackout and parliament" metaphor on p.54.)

"Her heart has slowed down and her blood pressure is low. She is having trouble when she moves from lying down to sitting up or standing," added Dr. Achebe.

---

9   In some programs that do not have a pediatrician or nurse on the team, the family doctor will provide the required medical information.

10   This is just one example of what an eating disorders assessment team might look like.

THE EARTHQUAKE-PROOF BUILDING

When we expect earthquakes, we construct our buildings lower and longer, to give them stability if the earth shakes.

It's like the body of a person with an eating disorder, which is more stable when she is lying down than when she is standing.

"She feels dizzy sometimes – she even told me she felt like she might faint at school during gym class yesterday," he said. (See "The half-full bottle" and Figure 3.6 on p.61.)

Dr. Achebe's voice became very serious: "Without attention now, Moira's low heart rate and blood pressure may continue to worsen and this could result in her death. Anorexia is a very serious illness. Up to 20 percent of people who get it eventually die from it or from its complications if it is not adequately managed. Not growing also means that Moira's bones are in danger of weakening. It is between the ages of 12 and 19 that bone density is laid down most intensely for girls. Moira's body will not put energy into bone development while it is conserving energy for her major internal organs, including the heart and brain."

THE BIG BAD WOLF AND THE HOUSE MADE OF STRAW

Strong bones are like walls that are made of bricks and mortar. Bones become weaker through starvation and malnutrition. Then they are more like bricks without mortar, or may even become more like straw. A bad wolf could blow them down with one puff. (See Figure 3.7 and "Osteoporosis and the brick wall" on pp.63–4.)

"Every vital organ is affected," Dr. Achebe continued. "Moira's brain is at risk because the teen years are a time of massive development of the brain, and this development will not occur as it is meant to without enough food to support it. Glucose is the brain's preferred energy source and it requires an uninterrupted supply, since it does not store any energy on its own. To use your brain, you need to keep it supplied with easily available glucose."

STOKING THE FIRE

Looking at Moira, Dr. Achebe asked her, "Do you know what our body temperature as human beings is supposed to be?"

Moira said, "Around 37° Centigrade or 98.7° Fahrenheit."

"That's right," said Dr. Achebe. "Now is that colder or hotter than it is outside most of the time?"

"It's hotter," answered Moira.

"Good, and what would you have to do to make the temperature around you go up to 37° Centigrade or 98.7 Fahrenheit?"

"Build a big fire."

"You are right. And to keep it at that temperature, would you have to keep putting logs on the fire, or could you just leave it for a day or two?"

"You would have to keep adding wood to keep the fire going," Moria said.

"Your body is the same," Dr. Achebe said. "You have to keep giving it food to keep the temperature up. Even when you are not active, when you are just resting, your body needs energy to keep itself at this temperature. Human beings are warm-blooded."

"I never thought about it that way," said Moira's brother, Alex. "No wonder you are always cold, Moira."

"I can't believe we have let this happen," said Moira's mother. She looked very uncomfortable as she looked at her husband. Then she looked at Dr. Achebe and said, "Please tell us you can help her."

"I'm glad you see how serious this is," he said, "and it is not your fault. You did not cause this to happen. But it is you, her parents, who are the ones who can help her. There is no person who can help her better than you."

Janine said, "Research shows that the most effective therapy for a teen who has anorexia is 'family-based therapy'. That means weekly meetings for your family with a family therapist who will coach you through the process of getting your daughter well. The therapist has expertise in eating disorders, but you are the experts on your daughter, especially when it comes to feeding her. You were able to feed her when she was little and needed to grow. You knew how to do this and what to give her. Now she needs you to help her with this again. Her life depends on your doing this."

Moira's dad asked, "Is there any medication you can prescribe that will help her, though?"

Dr. Achebe said, "Although in the literature there is some evidence to suggest that adults with bulimia nervosa may benefit from SSRIs,[11] there are no medications that are known to help directly with anorexia. Some medications like Prozac can help with depression or anxiety – you may have heard of this, but they may not work properly with someone like Moira, who has lost so much weight. It seems that the way these medications work depends on the presence of tryptophan (an essential amino-acid that usually comes from the food we eat) in the bloodstream, and it is known that tryptophan may not be as available when a person is in a semi-starved or starved state. The most essential thing that will help her right now is to have more food. And no one is in a better position than you and your wife to help her with that. For now, the most important thing is to help her get enough nutrition to support appropriate growth and development.[12] Sitting together at meals, serving her the amount you believe she needs, encouraging her in the ways you know best – you can get started today."

"And we will call you as soon as we have a family therapist available to assist you," said Janine, "It shouldn't be more than a few weeks. In the meantime, you should keep seeing your family doctor on a weekly basis. I will give you a form to take to her so she knows what information we need and can fax it to us after she sees you."[13]

Other outcomes of an assessment

Moira and her family are referred for outpatient therapy because Moira does not have any co-morbid conditions like severe anxiety or depression, she has been ill for a relatively short period of time, her family is not in the midst of serious conflict or divorce, and she is medically stable. These are good reasons to believe that Moira will be able to recover without an intervention that would interrupt her schooling and family life more than outpatient therapy,

---

11   This class of drugs includes fluoxetine, or Prozac, which has been shown through research to be helpful in preventing binge eating.

12   In this situation we are assuming that Moira is unlikely to be at risk of re-feeding syndrome based on the information the team has received from the medical doctor (see p.65).

13   The information needed from family physicians on a weekly basis includes: blood pressure lying and standing, heart rate lying and standing, weight, BMI, and date of last menstrual period. Every two weeks it is recommended that electrolytes, blood glucose, renal function, and amylase (if purging) be checked. Monthly, an ECG is recommended, and if the patient's BMI is less than 18, or she/he is purging, calcium, magnesium, phosphate, and albumin should be checked. Every four months, height should be taken. Every six months, LH and FSH should be checked if the patient is amenorrheic, and ferritin and sTSH should be checked if the patient is vegetarian or her/his BMI is less than 18. Annually, a bone density test should be done.

which will require her family to attend family therapy and medical checks once per week. Another option would be multi-family therapy (see Chapter 5), and the choice between single family or multi-family therapy could depend on staff availability or the perceived benefits of a group format over non-group format. For instance, families who are isolated or who have been trying but not succeeding in helping their child to recover, may benefit from working together with other families.

The assessment team would have considered referring Moira to a day hospital program (see Chapter 6) if Moira had shown signs of serious depression or anxiety and had been ill for a longer period of time with consequences to her physical health, like compromised bone density, significant lack of growth in height, or amenorrhea for more than six months. They would also have considered this if Moira and her family had already been working in outpatient therapy and not been able to make progress.

If Moira had attended the assessment and been medically compromised, the team would have referred her immediately to an inpatient unit, in a hospital with an available bed.

Outpatient family-based therapy (the Maudsley model)

In family-based therapy, the therapist provides expertise about eating disorders to parents so that they can take on the task of challenging the disordered eating behaviours of their child. The eating disorder is "externalized," which means that it is seen as separate from and having overtaken the child. This is a way of making the illness visible, so that parents can firmly but compassionately support their child to eat, rather than seeing her as stubborn or disobedient. It helps parents to separate their anger and frustration at the symptoms from their feelings for their children. Children and adolescents with eating disorders are not in control of the eating disorder behaviours and thoughts, and therefore need their parents to take charge of nutrition and weight restoration by managing meals and disrupting symptoms such as food restriction, over-exercising, and purging. The therapist helps keep the focus on restoring health. Parents respect the need for adolescents to exercise autonomy in areas not related to the eating disorder.

Family-based therapy has three phases: restoring weight so that it is consistent with the age and height expected for the individual; returning control over eating to the adolescent; and supporting the adolescent's developing autonomy (Lock *et al.* 2001).[14]

Phase 1: weight restoration

All members of the family living at home are expected to attend the family therapy sessions. There are roles for all family members in helping their child or sibling to get well. Often parents are "walking on eggshells" and feel angry, frustrated, guilty, and exhausted from trying to help the ill child, while the eating disorder doesn't budge or even gets stronger. Siblings may be angry or feel guilty, too, and may withdraw from the family into school and friends. Sometimes they take on a parental role in trying to get their sister or brother to eat, which is an inappropriate and costly burden for them (Jasper and Boachie 2007).

At the start, parents are asked to bring lunch, including a lunch that is sufficient to start reversing starvation in their ill child. This meal permits the therapist to see how the family is interacting around the eating disorder behaviours, and to assist the parents in getting their child to eat a little more than she was prepared to. The therapist emphasizes the necessity for the parents to be united against the eating disorder. The therapist coaches the family to recognize the "voice of the eating disorder" and direct their frustration at it rather than at their daughter/sibling, and helps them to understand how difficult it is for the ill adolescent to challenge that voice. The ill adolescent will eventually recognize the difference between her own voice and that of the eating disorder.

At home, it is crucial that the parents work together to ensure the child is supported to eat the required amount of food, at every meal and snack, and not to exercise or purge afterward. Siblings can help with distraction or supportive conversation without stepping into the

---

14 For further and detailed description of this treatment model, read James Lock and Daniel LeGrange (2005) *Help your Teenager Beat an Eating Disorder*. New York: The Guilford Press.

parental role. Families work out their own ways of following through with this necessary work. The therapist helps the family to persist and reinvigorates them to get past the frustration, anger, and despair that are normally part of the process of recovery, always guiding them to avoid criticism and judgement of the child, rather directing any anger and blame toward the eating disorder.

Phase 1 typically takes about ten sessions, but may take more. During this phase, family and developmental problems that are not directly related to eating disorder symptom management are purposely ignored. They are taken up in later phases. Phase 1 ends when parents' confidence in their ability to support their child's recovery is stable and the child is generally accepting of their parents' expectations at meals and is gaining weight steadily, so long as this is needed (Lock *et al.* 2001).

First outpatient therapy session

While she was putting lunch together to take to the first family session, Moira's mom, Stephanie, was imagining what it would be like trying to get Moira to eat the lunch. Maybe the therapist would show Stephanie how to manage it, or maybe she would have a magic wand to wave. In the three weeks since the assessment, Stephanie had been trying to get Moira to eat more and there had been some really awful scenes. One night Stephanie recalled coming close to hitting Moira. Just thinking about it was making Stephanie dread this family session. Would Moira start screaming at her right in front of the therapist, throw food at her, or would she just go silent, not budge, and not eat a single bite? Or...what if she were to eat the whole lunch without a single complaint? Then the therapist would think Stephanie was just incompetent.

The ring of the phone interrupted her thoughts. Stephanie picked up the phone. It was Moira's dad, Jake, saying there was a crisis at work and he doubted he would be able to get away at lunch to come to the session. Jake had been spending more and more time at work since the assessment. Stephanie tried to stay calm. She reminded Jake that the secretary had told her that all members of the family must attend this session.

Jake did not understand why he was needed in the middle of the workday to go to a lunch with his family. Stephanie and Moira were often fighting with one another at meals. Since it was between the two of them, he thought it made more sense for them to go to the therapist together. Theirs was a traditional family in terms of roles – it had suited them for Stephanie to stay home with the children and for him to stay at work. His income was the largest, and he wasn't as patient as Stephanie by nature. She had always looked after most of the meals. If it had been a regular day at work, Jake wouldn't have minded taking the time off – he understood that Moira was ill and he would like to see that the therapist was proficient – but now there had developed a crisis at work and he didn't feel right about leaving. To Stephanie he said, "Surely it will be all right if I go to the next meeting instead. I did just go to the assessment."

A few minutes later Stephanie called Jake back and said the secretary had told her that the whole family must come to the appointment. They could re-schedule if Jake were unable to attend. Jake said he would see what he could do.

Jake, Stephanie, Moira, and Alex arrived at the therapist's office with their picnic lunch in hand. Janine, the family therapist they had seen at the assessment, invited them in. Janine took Moira to a separate room to take her weight. She asked Moira to stand with her back to the numbers on the scale, so that she would not see her weight. Moira had lost some weight every week since her assessment, and this week was no different. When Janine and Moira came back to the family room, Janine let the rest of the family know. Stephanie's eyes filled with tears as she told Janine what it had been like trying to get Moira to eat more. Nothing had worked. Moira looked away. Janine explained how difficult it is for a young person to give up an eating disorder.

THE LEAKY RAFT

Can you imagine that your child is drowning in a massive sea and has only a poorly constructed raft to hold onto to keep herself above water? Although she knows the raft is leaking she convinces herself that it is the reason why she is still alive. You know that the water is carrying your child toward a dangerous waterfall not far away. A rescue helicopter is sent to dangle a rope for her to grab, but she has to let go of the raft to reach the rope. She has to risk losing the only thing buoying her up, and all she can see is a massive sea around her. She may refuse to do so, especially if she is afraid of heights. She will think, "What if I miss the rope?" If she refuses the rope, then the rescuers will be bewildered and may even get angry with her. (See Figure 4.3.)

Moira looked at her mom: "It really doesn't help when you get angry at me!" Stephanie said, "It's true Janine. I don't know what to do sometimes. It really feels like she's doing it on purpose, just refusing to eat, when she knows we are all trying to help her. I have gotten very frustrated. Looking at Moira, she said, "But Moira, you don't eat enough when I'm calm, either."

"I can't," Moira said, "My stomach hurts."

"I see that you've brought lunch with you," Janine said, "Will you put it out on the table over here? You can eat and help Moira with her lunch, too."

Moira sat beside her mom. Jake and Alex sat next to Stephanie. Moira started slowly eating some salad while the others bit into their sandwiches. After Moira had eaten most of the salad, Stephanie asked her to eat some of her sandwich. Moira took a tiny bite, then put the sandwich down. When Stephanie asked her to take another bite, Moira said, "I can't eat anymore. My stomach hurts. It always does when I eat too much. I told you." Moira looked like she was in real pain, her eyes pleading with her mother not to make her eat more.

Figure 4.3: The leaky raft
Drawing by Nadia and Zulaikhah Boachie 2011

"Well," Jake said, "there must be something wrong with her stomach. We can't push her to eat if it hurts her. Shouldn't we have a doctor look at her?"

"Moira's feelings are very real," said Janine, "but there may not be any organic reason for her stomach-ache. Your family doctor had that checked out before we started our meetings. Moira really needs more food. Without more food, her heart will get worse. Can you help her to have more food?"

THE STOMACH IS A MUSCLE

Blowing up balloons for a birthday party...it takes some effort to blow them up the first time, but it becomes easier if they deflate and are blown up again. If they are then put away and kept for another occasion, they will be difficult to blow up again. In this case the cheeks of the person inflating them may hurt, as it can require a lot more effort to re-inflate that balloon than the last time it was blown up.

The stomach is a muscle that may hurt when it starts working more after a time of less use.

"Just take some deep breaths, Moira," said Stephanie, "Maybe your tummy has tightened up because you are thinking you shouldn't eat. But the food is good and you need to eat it." Moira put down her sandwich and took some breaths. Then she took a few more bites.

"That's all I can eat," she said, putting the sandwich down again. "It's a huge sandwich. Mine is even bigger than Alex's."

Alex piped in, "Mine was the same size, Moira. I don't want your heart to get worse. Go ahead and eat it."

"It's the same as the day your friend Lara was over and had dinner with us. You were eating so little and were saying we gave you too much – more than anyone else. You say Lara has an eating disorder, but I saw her. She's not bony like you are and she ate a full dinner like the rest of us," Stephanie said.

"But do you know what she does?" Moira said. "She throws up after she's eaten. She eats a lot, sometimes bags and bags of cookies, but then she goes in the washroom and puts her finger down her throat to make herself throw up. So she doesn't really eat anything. You're making me eat way more than she does." As Moira finished her sentence, Stephanie looked horrified. She looked at Jake and than at Janine.

"That is a very risky practice – it may be that she has bulimia nervosa," said Janine. "Then your friend Lara needs help, too. Her weight may not be a medical issue, but the purging is very dangerous. It can also affect her heart. She could benefit by having a parent help her not to purge after meals."

Moira took another few bites. She had finished half of the sandwich. A tear rolled down her cheek and she said, "Ooohhh, my tummy is really hurting now." Stephanie looked at Jake and raised her eyebrows. Jake said, "If she is worried about eating, wouldn't it be better to help her settle her worries first than to make her eat? Wouldn't it be easier for her to eat, then?"

"Yes," Moira said, sounding relieved, "I think that would be better."

Janine said, "I wish I could tell you that it would be that way. Years of experience have shown us that working on the psychological issues alone doesn't make it easier to eat. It's far more likely to maintain Moira's eating disorder longer, and that could affect her bones, her vital organs, and her overall development. You are not giving Moira this lunch to punish her or to hurt her; it is really what her body needs. Once she is on the road to getting physically well, she will have opportunities to talk about her worries and anything else that is important to her. She won't be able to take advantage of those opportunities if she isn't doing better physically."

FEAR OF FLYING, A TICKET, AND A PASSPORT

If someone is afraid of flying and they must travel, you have to buy them a ticket for the travel date and make sure they have a valid passport. Then you work hard to help them at least reduce their anxiety so that they will agree to board the plane. Unless the person has the proper documents, they won't be able to get on the plane when it's time to go. There may not be any tickets left.

An eating disorder is partly physical and partly psychological. Usually, if the physical issues are not managed initially, it is more difficult to understand what the psychological aspects are, let alone help the person to deal with them.

Moira had set her sandwich on the paper plate in front of her. She looked at her dad and then frowned at Janine. "This is stupid," Moira raised her voice, "Don't listen to her. She doesn't know what she's talking about. You've never made me eat before when I had a stomach-ache. I'm not eating any more!"

Jake said, "Moira, that's enough. You are being rude to Janine. She's trying to help us. He apologized to Janine, "I'm sorry, Moira doesn't usually say things like that."

"You can think of it as anorexia talking," said Janine. "Other parents notice the same thing. Their child is calm and content and polite as long as it's not time for a meal or snack. Then, when they start to support their child to eat enough food, it's like the anorexia is threatened and lashes out to get them to back off."

Jake looked at Janine and asked, "What can we do? We can't force her to eat."

Janine pointed to a chair and said, "Jake why don't you try sitting over there?" Jake got up and moved, so that Moira was sitting between him and Stephanie.

Jake said to Moira, "You don't need to be scared. Your mom and I will help you. Even if it hurts your tummy when you eat right now, it is the right thing to do. We want you to finish the whole sandwich."

"It's okay, Moira. Remember, I ate one too," said Alex.

Moira finished her sandwich while Alex told some stories about things that were happening at school. With a little more support she drank her milk as well.

Janine encouraged the family to continue working together to support Moira at meals and snacks. She observed that Alex had contributed a lot just by doing the things a brother can do – encouraging Moira, reminding her that it is okay to eat, and telling her he cares about her. Moira said that she liked it when he told stories from school because it made things feel more normal and she didn't feel like all the attention was on her. Stephanie agreed that it had been helpful to have Alex there, but that she did not want him to think it was his responsibility. Janine agreed and reflected that Stephanie and Jake working together seemed to have given Moira the strength to finish her whole lunch. Jake said he had learned more about the eating disorder by coming to the meeting. He hadn't realized how difficult it could be for Moira to eat.

STRENGTH THROUGH UNITY

Why do we bother marrying and working hard to stay married, hoping it will be for the rest of our lives? Staying single does not mean you cannot raise a child. Parents who are single by choice or circumstance do it all the time, but it is easier if there is more than one adult. Perhaps it is the fact that each parent brings unique qualities, each of which their children may need. Neither parent is better than the other, and a child may inherit different aspects of each. When parents work together to help a child, even if they are divorced, their combined qualities and a unity of purpose can defeat many troubles, including an eating disorder.

Janine said, "It may get more difficult before it gets better." She described how the intensity of Moira's protests might increase as they challenged her eating disorder symptoms. It was this protest they had seen at lunch when Moira made an outburst that seemed uncharacteristic of her.

"If you keep supporting Moira to eat so that she can fight the eating disorder, eventually she will get well, and then she will be presenting you with the usual teenage issues like curfews and such."[15]

---

15 See the detailed discussion of the stages of illness and recovery as shown in Figure 8.1 on p.153.

HOW LONG DOES IT TAKE?

Nobody knows. It is like when your child learned to walk. Some children start earlier and some start later. Your job was to feed her, make sure she got rest, play with her, encourage her, and so on. Even though you did not know when she would walk, you knew that eventually she would, so you kept on doing all the things that would contribute to her walking, over and over again.

Stephanie and Jake looked tired but pleased as they left the office with Moira and Alex. Stephanie felt more hopeful than she had felt in a long time. Moira asked Alex if he would play with her when they got home.

When Janine was reflecting on the session later in the day, she thought that Stephanie had been relieved to know what to expect and to have some ideas about how to handle the meals. Janine wondered, though, whether Jake really believed that Moira would behave in the ways predicted. She might not have done enough to get across to him what kind of an illness an eating disorder is, and he might be thinking that she just didn't understand the kind of person Moira is. Still, Janine was satisfied that Jake and Stephanie could work in a united way to support Moira, and so she felt hopeful that the therapy would be successful.

Second outpatient therapy appointment

It was therapy day again and Stephanie couldn't remember why she had felt hopeful last week. Except for breakfast, it had been non-stop arguing with Moira about everything she put in front of her to eat. Moira wasn't complaining as much about stomach-aches, though she still had them, but there was almost nothing she liked to eat. How many extra trips to the grocery store had Stephanie made this week to get something Moira said she would like better? She'd lost count. And then there was all the negotiating about when and where Moira would eat. Stephanie was sure she'd gotten more food into Moira at breakfasts and lunches, but after that, Moira was constantly saying she was too full and she would have some of her food later, or she would take it up to her room to have while she did her homework. Stephanie wasn't sure that was a good idea, but she'd agreed with Jake when he said they should give Moira a chance. He believed Moira had gotten the point at the last meeting and would eat now that she knew she had to.

Prior to meeting the family, Janine looked over the most recent fax she had received from Dr. Chau. Moira's vitals were about the same as the previous week. There were no alarms according to the lab work Dr. Chau had ordered. As Janine greeted the family in the waiting area, she sensed there was tension among them. She took Moira's weight. The scale showed the same number as the previous week. Moira had not lost more weight, but she had not gained any either.

After letting the family know about this, Janine said, "What do you think contributed to her not losing any weight this week? What went well?" Stephanie said that she had arranged for Moira to have her lunch in the guidance counselor's office at school. Moira had cried that it wasn't fair and she was missing time with her friends, but Stephanie had stayed firm. Janine asked what might be needed now to help Moira gain weight.

"I don't need to gain weight!" shouted Moira, "My heart is okay now. Dr. Chau said so. I won't lose any more. I promise."

"Why does she need to gain weight?" challenged Jake, "She seems to be an okay weight to me. She's only 14 and we're not big people in our family. You can see that." Janine suggested it might be something they would like to discuss further with Dr. Chau, who had known Moira since she was born, but that she would gladly go over some of the principles.

"At 14, Moira is just at the beginning of a time when it is natural for her to have a spurt of growth, including height. In order to support this growth in height, she needs to gain some weight first, so that her body will sense that it can put energy into supporting her growth including getting taller, that it doesn't have to conserve every bit of energy to protect only her vital organs," explained Janine. "Remember, she hasn't gotten her menstrual periods back yet, either."

"And," Stephanie added, looking at Moira, "Dr. Chau said your vitals are no worse today, she didn't say you are all better or that your heart is out of danger."

"How much does she need to gain, then?" asked Jake.

Janine said, "Dr. Chau can help you more with the specifics, but it's good to think of a growing teen's weight as a "moving target." While adults' weights may not need to change much over time (apart from pregnancy), children and adolescents are growing. They will weigh more when they are taller than they do when they are younger and shorter."

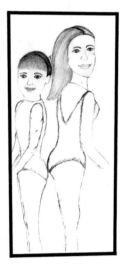

Figure 4.4: Effects of eating disorders on growth
The drawings depict twins at ages 3 and 13, one of whom developed
an eating disorder and did not grow as tall as her sister
Drawings by Zaleekhah Boachie 2011

PROGRESS WEIGHT

A young woman who has not yet started menstruating, or who has not reached her full height, thinks that her weight is normal. She doesn't want to gain weight, so she won't stop exercising and/or she won't eat enough food to gain. She's afraid she'll "blow up" in weight. She doesn't realize that she must continue eating normally and may need to exercise less, otherwise her period will never come or won't resume. She won't reach her full height. Unlike a fully-grown adult, her weight is a "moving target" and it is not safe for her to restrict food intake.

As Figure 4.5 on the following page shows, if you shoot directly at the moon, you'll miss it, because it's moving.

"There you go, Moira," said Jake, "That's why you need to gain more. We can't let you just stay at this weight." Stephanie scanned her memory of the week, looking for times that Moira might have missed eating what she was supposed to.

Figure 4.5: Shooting at the moon
Drawing by Nadia Boachie 2011

"Moira, I thought you said that you'd eaten the food you took upstairs after dinner. I asked you and you said that you did," she said. "I hope you weren't lying to me about that."

"It was 'eaten.' You didn't ask if it was 'all eaten.' I gave some to Freckles. He was way hungrier than I was, because you forgot to feed him!" Moira cried.

BEING ECONOMICAL WITH THE TRUTH

Did you eat your lunch? Yes.

Was anyone watching you? Yes.

Was Dad here? Yes.

She ate an amount she was comfortable with, but not sufficient according to her meal plan, while her companion dog watched her and eagerly ate the cast-offs. Dad was in the house, but an important call came in just as lunch started and he had to take it. She isn't lying, but is being "economical with the truth."

"Well," said Jake, "I thought we could give you a chance, Moira, to show us you could handle this responsibility. I thought you had really understood last week when we talked about how you have to eat, even if your tummy hurts. But clearly you can't be trusted on this."

"Jake, it isn't her fault. Normally you could trust her and at her age it's the right thing to do to give her chances to show she can be trusted. But this is an illness, and the eating disorder will not let her tell you more than absolutely necessary. It's really the eating disorder that you can't trust right now," said Janine. "You can help Moira by asking her very direct and clear questions. Previously she would have answered to the spirit of your questions, but with this illness, she will be able to answer only to the letter of them, especially if it gives the eating disorder an 'out'."

"Do you think we should let her eat on her own at home?" asked Jake.

"There will come a time when Moira will be able to handle responsibility for her own meals again. But at this stage, it would be better if you were to keep her company and check that she's eaten everything she needs at each meal or snack," said Janine. "If she doesn't have everything, she'll get behind and then she'll end the day in a deficit and she won't get to the weight her body needs." (See "Paying off a credit card" on p.120.)

"I have a question," said Stephanie, "Moira has been asking for other foods than the ones I've prepared. She doesn't seem to like our typical family foods anymore. But the more I change things for her, the more she seems to ask for changes. What should I do?"

"We find that it's most helpful if there are limited choices for a particular meal," answered Janine, "You can plan meals in advance and give Moira some input into what will be included at each meal, but base the choices you give her on what foods you normally prepare and what you know she needs to have. Once you've agreed on a plan, it's best to stick with that plan and not negotiate last-minute changes. If you negotiate last-minute changes, Moira will feel doubts about what she has chosen and she'll get anxious about whether she chose the right thing. Then it will be the eating disorder that is making suggestions, and it cannot be trusted to help Moira get what she needs. You are her parents. You have always known what to feed Moira to keep her healthy."

This work of assisting the family to help Moira eat sufficient food without compensation, so that she gains weight as needed, is repeated until there are signs that Moira is taking responsibility for her own food intake. This usually takes about four to six months.

Phases 2 and 3 of outpatient family-based therapy

Phase 2 is the process of returning control of food intake to the adolescent. Parents begin the shift from being "on their child's back" to "watching her back." Phase 2 starts with a discussion of "how did we succeed in arriving here," which is a review of what parents, siblings, and the teen have done that have helped them to make progress. As long as the teen's weight is continuing to move toward full restoration, parents can encourage her re-engagement with social and other activities that may have been interrupted by the eating disorder. The therapist helps the family work out solutions to issues that come up. If a teen asks to go with friends to a restaurant, they may agree, but ask her to review the menu with them in advance and choose what she will order. The therapist also works with the teen during this time to help her continue to distinguish her own voice from that of the eating disorder, and watches for the re-emergence of issues that may have contributed to the development of the eating disorder. For example, depression, anxiety, body image issues, family relationship issues, or undisclosed abuse may surface at this time (or later). This phase lasts about two to three months and meetings may move from weekly to every two weeks (Jasper, Boachie and Lafrance 2009; Lock *et al.* 2001).

Phase 3 is primarily concerned with supporting the teen's developing autonomy. It starts when the teen's weight is stable (or continuing to rise, if she is continuing to grow in height) and is no longer in a self-starving mode of thinking. Therapy sessions may occur just once a month and are focused on issues related to identity and autonomy, like leaving home for college, social independence, and sexuality. At this time, parents are encouraged to start re-organizing their life as a couple: to do things together or begin projects they have been putting off. Therapy ends around this time (Jasper *et al.* 2009; Lock *et al.* 2001).

It is important to note that the three phases of the therapy process do not proceed in a linear fashion (see Figure 4.6). There may be many occurrences of slipping into eating disorder behaviours again. These require a quick response on the part of parents to go back to earlier levels of support, and then when the teen can manage more on her own, to move to less stringent support again (Jasper *et al.* 2009; Lock *et al.* 2001).

Not like this:

Like this:

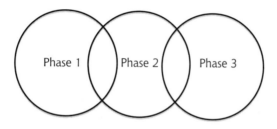

Figure 4.6: Overlapping phases of recovery

Chapter 5

Multi-family
Therapy

Like single-family therapy for eating disorders, multi-family therapy uses family-based principles, also known as the Maudsley model. Parents are coached to be united in supporting their children to eat without compensating, and to accept any weight gain required to put them back on their developmental paths. What is different in multi-family therapy is that it combines professional expertise with a community of support made up of other families dealing with the same or very similar illnesses. Parents can draw strength from other families in the group and draw on the expertise that exists among them.

Up to eight families attend, with children who are at different stages of recovery from an eating disorder. It helps parents, especially, to see that they are not to blame for the eating disorder, when they are with other families and see that there is no one type of family in which eating disorders develop: all kinds of family constellations are represented, all religions, and all economic groups. Those who are at an earlier stage see that progress is possible. When parents see that other parents share their frustrations and challenges, they find it easier to be less critical of themselves.

The first meeting of multi-family therapy is an introductory evening. Prospective families meet the staff and each other. An expert in eating disorders gives a presentation about the nature and long-term effects of eating disorders, highlighting the reasons why it is urgent to help one's child recover and prevent the disorder from becoming chronic. A guest family who have previously completed a multi-family group also attend, and share their experience of the program and answer questions.

About a week after the introductory evening, there is a four-day intensive session attended by all members of each family. Every day there are two snacks and a meal. Families support one another and are supported by staff to help their children to eat. In addition, there are opportunities for discussion in small groups: for parents to share the challenges and frustrations they experience during mealtimes; for the teens to express through drawing, modeling clay, or collage, what it is like to have an eating disorder; and for siblings to share and write about their perspective on life with an eating disorder in the family. Later, these creative works are shared in the large group. Teens can see the impact of the eating disorder on their siblings, and parents and siblings can appreciate the extent to which the affected teens feel trapped, seduced, and hurt by the eating disorder. These and other activities help family members share their perspectives with one another, allowing for increased compassion and deeper understanding of each other, as well as increased visibility of the effects of the eating disorder. Seeing things differently and being more open, group members are able to try creative solutions to problems. Family members who don't blame each other are better able to work together against the eating disorder. Difficulties can be taken on in solidarity with the other group members and successes can be shared and celebrated in the group (Eisler 2005; Jasper, Boachie and Lafrance 2010; Scholz *et al.* 2005).

What does it look like?

CASE EXAMPLE: TIM

Warren was sitting in the circle with his wife Abby, their two children, Nora and Tim, between them. He looked around the room. It was the third day of multi-family group and he was hoping that today he would get what he came for: some solutions to the problem of Tim's eating disorder. Nearly everyone had arrived; the activities would start soon.

Warren was surprised to find himself feeling concerned that the Schaeffer family had not yet arrived. They'd had a very difficult time getting through lunch the day before. After learning that their daughter Kayla had been vomiting after meals for about three months, George and Freda had given her a choice: either she could go to the washroom on her own before lunch, or she would be accompanied to the washroom if she were to go after lunch. It was like a switch had been turned off. Kayla refused to eat more than half of the lunch they'd brought for her. They'd asked for support from the staff and other families, and Kayla eventually ate more.

Warren had admired how persistent George and Freda had been. Before he saw that, he would have insisted that he and Abby had tried everything. Now he wondered if they were giving up too easily. It was a surprise to hear George talking openly in the parent group later about how angry he'd been with Kayla. Warren wasn't sure he would have acknowledged feelings like that in a group; he worried about others judging him, but he sure had felt anger toward Tim. And, although he felt guilty for it, Warren also felt relieved that someone else's kid was purging. Having a boy with a "girl's illness" often made him feel ashamed. Even here he felt out of place. Until Kayla admitted that she was purging, Warren thought Tim was the only one in the room doing that.

Warren's gaze swept the circle of chairs. It was really astounding how different from one another all these families were and yet how similar their predicament. There was the single mom with twins and an older daughter; one of the twins was ill. There was the man Warren thought he recognized from television with his wife, and their daughter who had been anorexic for two years or more. There was a brother or sister, too, but older and living away at university. Clearly money couldn't protect a family from an eating disorder. Then there was the couple who appeared to be teenagers themselves; until you saw that they had two teenage kids. The older one was the one with anorexia. Finally, there was the family who seemed like the most ordinary family in the world: mom, dad, and three kids aged 15, 12, and 8. Their 15-year-old was ill with anorexia. Just as Warren finished looking around the circle, the Schaeffers walked in and the day began.

The family sculpt

Paula, one of the group facilitators, explained that the next group activity was called "Family sculpt" (Asen and Scholz 2010, pp.66–8) and it would help the families see the impact of the eating disorder on their family and get a feel for what would be needed to move the eating disorder out. Paula looked at Tim and invited him to come to the centre of the circle with her.

"Select a member from the group to represent each of your family members, and then arrange them inside the circle here," said Paula. Tim found a group member for each of his family members who agreed to stand in the circle with him.

"Arrange them in a way that shows how your family was at a time before the eating disorder arrived. Think about who is looking at whom, who is closer to others, and who is further away. Find a typical posture and position for each of them, or a movement if that is typical. They can move any way that you want them to, but they cannot talk. It is a kind of portrait of your family before the eating disorder."

Tim placed his "mother" and "father" close together and asked them to look sweetly at their children, who were to the right of their mother. He asked his "sister" and "Tim" to face each other and act like they were playing and talking together. Then he said that his "mother" and "father" should take turns entering and exiting the family space, pausing to join in and play with their children before entering or exiting again. "There," Tim said, "that's it." Paula asked the group members who were standing in for Tim's family to enact his instructions for a minute, then to stand quietly in their positions and allow themselves to experience how they felt. When she asked them to describe how it felt being in this family, the "mom" said that it felt a little chaotic, but at the same time it felt loving and fun. The other family members felt similarly. When Paula asked Tim and his real family members about whether the sculpt fit with how they remembered their family before the eating disorder, they said it was reflected well.

Paula then asked Tim to re-sculpt the family to portray it in the present. Tim placed the family members as though they were around a big dinner table. His "sister" was sitting beside him and his "mom" was sitting at the other side of the table. His "dad" stood at the edge of the dining room to represent his being sometimes there and sometimes away on business travel. Tim instructed his "mom" to pick up a cell phone and talk into it for a while, then to put it down again.

Paula said, "Now, Tim, choose a person to represent the eating disorder. It should be a staff person, not anyone from the families here." Tim chose Morris.

"Position Morris, 'The Eating Disorder,' in a way that shows us your relationship with him. Where is he in relation to you? Is he standing, sitting, or moving? Is he above you or beside you, or at your feet? What kind of manner does he have? Let Morris know how he should talk to you in order to sound the way the eating disorder does. When you are ready, give your 'family members' instructions about how they should act as we put this sculpt into action." Tim thought for a moment, then spoke quietly to the others inside the circle with him.

"Okay, we're ready," he said.

Paula said, "Get into your starting places and on the count of three, go into action." She waited while they placed themselves, then said, "One...two...three...action."

"Tim," his "mom" and "sister" acted out a normal dinner-table scene, while "dad" hovered near the edge of the room. "Mom's" cell phone rang and she picked it up. Then "Tim" got up and said he had to go to wrestling practice. "Sister" said to "Tim," "Go straight to your practice – you promised me." As "Tim" walked away, "The Eating Disorder" started walking beside him.

It said very harshly, "You ate too much. You'll never make your weight category now. Friday is the competition and you won't make it. You're weak. You're a loser. Nothing but a loser." Then it jumped in front of him and said in a drug-dealer voice, "Hey man, you can redeem yourself. Just make yourself puke and it'll be a new game."

"Tim" looked around. He couldn't catch anyone's eye. He looked doubtful. Then "The Eating Disorder" put his arm around "Tim" and led him away.

Tim's "mom" put the telephone down, looked up at his "sister" and said, "Oh, did Tim leave for practice already?"

Paula said, "OK, stop action!"

As they debriefed the sculpt, the actors talked about their experience doing it. "Dad" said he was aware of being so far outside of what was happening in his family that he didn't know his son was in trouble. He felt sad. "Mom" felt uneasy, but didn't quite know why. Tim was gone by the time she looked up. "Sister" said she was feeling helpless as she saw "The Eating Disorder" sidle up to "Tim," but couldn't say anything to her parents because she had promised Tim she wouldn't, just as he had promised her he would stop purging.

Paula invited Tim, Warren, Abby, and Nora to comment. "I felt sad watching it," said Warren, "There's something about seeing it played out like this. I mean, in reality it's not quite so cut and dried, but there's a core truth in there. It really hit me hard, watching it. Tim and I used to do stuff together, and since I started this job where I travel a lot, I haven't even seen any of his competition matches in almost a year."

"For me," said Abby when Paula looked at her, "I don't know. I knew something was wrong, but I didn't know what. It wasn't till Tim collapsed at a match and was taken to hospital that I discovered what it was. Nora should have told us. She's the only one who knew."

"I couldn't!" said Nora. "Tim would have hated me, and anyway he kept promising me he would stop and then he told me he had stopped. So I didn't know he was going to collapse!"

"I was planning to stop. I meant it when I said it. I didn't know that puking could do damage," said Tim.

Paula looked at Morris, "The Eating Disorder," and said, "What about you?"

Morris said, "For me it was easy as pie. I got at him when he was the most vulnerable – after a meal, alone, and thinking about winning or losing at wrestling. Then I knew just what to say to him to get him to go along with me."

Paula said, "Okay. I want all of you who have been playing Tim's family members to shake off your roles and take on your own identities again. Just shake it off and come back to yourself." They did.

"Warren, Abby, and Nora...if you are willing, come and join Tim in the circle here. We're going to have you play out the same scene. Only this time, you should do everything and anything you can think of to get Tim away from 'The Eating Disorder.' Do any of you feel that you would prefer to have another group member take your place? Take your time."

All of Tim's family members were willing to try it out. They set up the same scene that had just been played out. Morris continued as "The Eating Disorder." As Tim got up from the table to go to wrestling practice, Nora looked at him.

Abby put down her phone and said, "Go after him. He trusts you." Nora got up and went after Tim. Tim stopped and reassured her that he was going straight to wrestling. As they talked, the Eating Disorder kept its distance and only moved in closer as Tim got further away from his family.

Paula said, "Look, the Eating Disorder is after him again! What are you going to do?"

"I'm supposedly on a business trip. I can't do anything from here," said Warren.

"He's 16. He won't listen to his mother," said Abby, "I don't know what I can do besides get Nora to talk to him."

"It's not working this way, though. Not for anyone but 'The Eating Disorder,' said Paula sadly, "It's taking off with your only son. You've got to think of something!" The family floundered for a little while longer.

"Okay" Warren said, "I've got a cell phone, he's got a cell phone. I'll call him. Abby, go after him. I'll phone him and tell him why you are going to drive him back home. Nora, you go with your mom and help her. Distract him from 'The Eating Disorder' while she gets him in the car!"

As they played it out, and Tim got the phone call from his dad, "The Eating Disorder" escalated its efforts to criticize and seduce him. It raised its voice. Tim looked confused. Nora took his hand and led him toward their mother. Then Abby said in a voice no one in the room had previously heard her use, "If you don't get in the car, you will die. That is not going to happen. Get in now."

Tim stepped into the car and Nora quickly bolted the locks. "The Eating Disorder" tried, but could not get in. It called after them, "That's only Round One. I'm going to fight you for him."

Paula gathered the family together in the centre again. They looked exhausted but pleased. Tim was smiling. "Okay," she said, "tell us how that was."

Tim said, "I don't think any one of those things my family did would have worked without the others. I wouldn't have listened to any of them, especially with 'The Eating Disorder' saying what it was saying to me. When they all got together like that, it was different."

"I'm going to have to find a way not to be traveling so often," Warren said, "It's a terrible feeling to be so far away when your child is being kidnapped."

Nora said, "It felt such a relief to have my mom and dad helping me."

"I don't know," said Abby, "It doesn't feel right telling a 16-year-old boy what to do."

"Any comments about this sculpt from group members?" Paula asked, looking out to the circle.

Kayla's mother said, "Abby, maybe you couldn't see it from where you were standing, but there was a point there when Tim looked really confused, like for a while he couldn't find a way to decide what to do. You won't have to tell him forever...just until he can make healthier decisions for himself again in this area. There are probably lots of things that Tim makes great choices about on his own."

"Yes, that's true. I didn't think about it that way," said Abby.

"How did 'The Eating Disorder' feel this time?" Paula asked Morris.

"I was very annoyed. I don't like losing, but I was outnumbered. I'm definitely going to look for a comeback opportunity," Morris replied.

"We're nearly done, but there is one more piece to the sculpt," Paula said, "This is the part where you look into the future and portray your family the way you would like things to be a year or two from now."

Tim brought his dad closer to the rest of his family members. He stood his mother and father looking at each other. He put himself and Nora a little apart from them and then decided that Nora might be away at university and put her about ten feet from the rest of the family, but looking toward them.

Paula asked, "What about 'The Eating Disorder'? Where will it be?" Tim paused to think for a while, then directed "The Eating Disorder" to stand outside the circle and behind his family, where it could not be seen by any of them.

"Does it feel like 'The Eating Disorder' is still a threat there?" asked Paula.

"More like a memory. I'd like it to be just a memory by then," answered Tim. "So I can see it if I look for it, but it's not coming at me anymore."

Families make progress in helping their teens to eat and in limiting other eating disorder symptoms over the four days of the intensive. Parents learn from their children what it is like to have an eating disorder and how trapped they feel. Just as with the analogy "When individual rights and parental responsibility collide" (p.21), parents learn that there are times when they have to take over. The children learn that their parents know more than they thought they did and that they are able to help them. They also learn that their siblings feel for them, are angry at the eating disorder, and are willing to lend a hand. Siblings are relieved of any parental-type responsibilities they may have taken on and are free to be children or teenagers again.

Timelines

The final activity of the four days is called "Timelines." Each family, separately, plans the time ahead, leading up to the point when the eating disorder will be out of their lives. On a large piece of paper they work back to the present, plotting in critical events, threats, and strategies month-by-month on the one hand, and on the other hand, achievements, goals, and progress with weight. Each family chooses for their timeline a symbolic form that suits them: a river, a road, a circle, a chart, a mountain, and so on. The timelines may be detailed or more impressionistic, depending on how the family processes information. The teens generally find it difficult to commit to a time when the eating disorder is out of their lives, and there may be conflict with parents who want them to commit to a time, preferably an earlier one. The activity lets parents know that although the teens are not at all ready to take back full responsibility for feeding themselves or for letting go of the benefits the eating disorder has provided, there is hope, because they have succeeded in helping their teens to increase their food intake and decrease other symptoms, communication among family members has increased, and their strengths as a family have been effective.

First follow-up day after multi-family intensive

On the first follow-up day, two weeks after the intensive, families check in with one another about how the previous two weeks have been. They share positive changes they've maintained since the last session: adding a snack, including more milk, or supervising bathroom use after meals. In spite of the progress, they may still be frustrated and discouraged because they had hoped it would be easier to make faster progress. The eating disorder is still in control. One or two families are invited to do "family sculpts" – each finding their own way to deal with the externalized or symbolic eating disorder. Morning snack and lunch provide opportunities for families to use the group and staff support to help their teens have more to eat without compensating. The main activity of the afternoon is "Treasures and Traps," an activity that is symbolic of the process of recovery from an eating disorder.

Treasures and Traps

For this activity, the room is radically changed in format from the usual circle of chairs that defines the discussion space. All the chairs are pushed out of the way to the edges of the room. Masking tape is used to delineate a very large rectangle on the floor. Within the rectangle, dollars and dollars of play money – or "treasure" – are scattered. Amidst the play money, there are lots of paper cups – or "traps" – turned upside down.

On one side of the rectangle, behind the masking-tape line, all of the teens line up and are blindfolded. Opposite each teen, on the other side of the rectangle, is one of their parents, whose job it is to guide them across the rectangle, using only the parent's voice. The idea is to guide the teens to pick up as much money as they can and avoid the traps as they cross the floor. Touching a cup, or even just brushing against one with a hand or a shoe, results in forfeiting all the money gathered up to that point, and going back to the beginning. Volunteers, usually siblings, help the staff to referee by standing along the sidelines, watching for paper cup violations. The referees are strict and a teen crossing the rectangle is "safe" only after both feet are across the masking-tape line behind which their parent is standing. Only when all the teens have completed their crossings does this part of the activity end. The teens record on a flip chart the amount of money they have gathered along the way, and the game is played again with the roles reversed. Parents wear the blindfolds and are guided across by their teens. A final game gives siblings the opportunity to try it out as well.

Having three crossings allows for multiple perspectives, a key benefit of multi-family groups. Parents, teens, and siblings can see what it is like to be in one another's shoes: leading, being led, and being on the sidelines. At the end of the activity, plenty of debriefing time is allowed for group members to reflect on their experiences. They are encouraged to draw connections with the process of recovering from an eating disorder and are able to build up their understanding of this process as they hear each other's perspectives and feedback.

A central theme is "guiding and being guided in the midst of noise and chaos." At the start of "Treasures and Traps" the room becomes extremely noisy, and since no one has had time to develop a strategy for making progress, there is chaos and frustration. So it is with an eating disorder. Parents are trying to help their children to eat and not compensate for eating, in a world that surrounds them with messages that encourage dieting, weight loss, and body-shaping practices as the means to acceptance and success. The media, peers, teachers, coaches, and relatives may all be expressing these same messages. How are the children to hear their parents' voices in the midst of this constant noise? In the group activity, parents persist and find a way to help their children all the way across the floor. Different things work for different families. Some start very slowly, until they've established a mutual understanding that works – for example, how big is a "big step" supposed to be? Patience is crucial. Once communication is established, they can speed up. Some families whose first language is not English start speaking in their original language and the communication becomes easier: the teen can distinguish her parent's voice more easily from the rest. Teens realize that the only way they can finish the activity is to listen for their parent's voice and trust it. No one has been seen to finish the crossing without this trust. And parents cannot do the crossing for their child; it must be accomplished through persistently communicating with them and entrusting them with the task. This includes staying behind the masking tape and watching while their children knock over cups, then helping them recover and learn from the mistake as they start again.

RECOVERY PROCESS AND THE GPS

You get into your car with your new GPS device mounted on the dashboard. You start the car, turn on the GPS, key in the address you are headed for, and follow the instructions. You start driving and make turns, prompted by the GPS. One of the prompts seems vague and you make a turn. It's the wrong turn and you hear the GPS voice say: "Recalculating...!" then it gives you new instructions. You are still going to the address you originally set out for, but now you are using a slightly different route. You go through this process as many times as needed until you get to your destination.

Recovering from an eating disorder requires frequent recalculating of strategy along the way.

"Expect setbacks" is another theme. Although a teen may have to go back to the start after knocking into a cup, she is not starting all over. She has the benefit of knowing better how to communicate with her parent, and can get back to the point where she stopped more quickly the second time, having learned from what went wrong the first time. It is similar with setbacks and relapses with eating disorders.

There can be different kinds of learning along the way. Some parents focus almost exclusively on getting across the floor without making a mistake and don't pick up money along the way. They may not notice till the end and see the treasure other families have gathered that focusing on perfection has a cost. It's possible to be effective in picking up money as well as finishing, even including some episodes of going back to the start.

Alternatively, parents may focus on getting all the treasure that is possible and thereby get distracted from the need to cross the finish line. They may give in to their child's demands to return to competitive sports, or stop supervising their meals, too soon, anxious to get her back amongst her peers, so that she won't miss anything.

POLICE STOP YOU FOR SPEEDING

When someone is speeding in a car and is stopped by the police they might be genuinely confused if they have no speedometer, or may be angry because they did not feel they were going too fast and hadn't looked at their speedometer. The same person, standing by the side of the road watching the cars go by, can easily see that some are going too fast.

A young person with an eating disorder may not appreciate the nature of her illness and what she may need to do to recover from it. She needs someone else, preferably a parent, to appreciate this for her.

The theme of "leading or being led" is a significant one. During the debriefing, staff will ask the teens whether they prefer leading their parents or being led by them. To the surprise of many parents, the teens typically say that they prefer to be led. It is easier and does not include the pressure of being responsible for another person. After this exercise, the teens are easier to lead: they realize that their parents are working hard and they appreciate the difficulties involved in leading. It helps them when they know they have someone they trust leading them through it.

The theme "How long will it take?" is also a common one. The activity doesn't end until everyone finishes. It can take a long time for some and not so long for others. Patience, communication, and allowing for setbacks all help the teens complete the game. However, no one can predict how long it will take for any one teen to finish.

HOW LONG WILL IT TAKE?

When your child sets out learning to drive, you cannot know how long it will take for her to get her driver's license. When she turns 16 she can start. You can help her study for the initial test that permits her to drive with a licensed driver in the car, but she may need to take the test more than once. After getting her learner's permit, she may be ready to drive on her own before eight months have passed or after, but the soonest she will be allowed to qualify for her license is after a minimum eight months. You pay for her driving lessons. You sit in the car with her as she practices over and over again. When she is ready for her final test, you drive her to the test place. She may pass the first time or not until the third time. Nobody can predict how long it will take. But you know that one day she will pass.

The "Treasures and Traps" activity is a powerful metaphor for understanding key aspects of the process of recovery from an eating disorder: working as a team, the essential need for trust, the need for communication and sharing of information, and the value of community.

After the first follow-up session, the multi-family group meets for one day approximately every two months for a year. As the year unfolds, the group leaders bring in activities and discussion points that are designed to help the families move along the stages of recovery. Between group sessions, families meet as needed with their individual family therapist and may or may not organize meetings with one another. The final session is designed entirely by the families themselves, a symbolic way of returning full responsibility to them. By the end of the year, some teens may be eating well on their own, needing minimal or no supervision by their parents and working actively toward autonomy.

Chapter 6

Day Hospital Program

The majority of eating disorders are managed on an outpatient basis with weekly clinic appointments, but with some teens this type of management may not be sufficient to allow them to fully recover. Lengthy inpatient stays could provide the needed structure and support, but are very expensive.[16] Because the day hospital program philosophy may include allowing participants to go home in the evenings and on the weekends, it provides an intermediate level of intervention with many advantages over long inpatient stays. Besides being far less expensive, day hospital programs provide greater family contact and support; increased connection with friends, school, and work; greater exposure to triggering situations, which fosters more opportunity to develop coping skills; a more positive group milieu than is usually found in an inpatient unit; and are conducive to the transfer of therapeutic gains to the home environment (Zipfel *et al.* 2002). At the same time, day programs provide structure and daily support that are not available through weekly outpatient clinic visits.

Day hospital programs may vary in focus, depending on local practice and on which profession is in the primary decision-making position: they can focus primarily on supporting weight gain/stabilization

---

16 Inpatient daily costs are about three to four times those of a day hospital (National Collaborating Centre for Mental Health and National Institute for Clinical Excellence 2004; Zipfel *et al.* 2002).

or they can focus on supporting both weight gain/stabilization and psychological change. They can function as a closed group, where all the patients start and end the program together, or as an open group, where patients start and end the program individually.

In this chapter, a Canadian day hospital program is described. It is headed by a psychiatrist. In other programs pediatricians or psychologists play the lead role, while in others there may be a shared care model. Our program uses an open group model and is designed to support both weight gain/stabilization and psychological change. Teens may be referred to our day program directly from an assessment. Alternatively, they may be stepping down from an inpatient stay or stepping up from weekly outpatient treatment. They must be medically stable, because they go home every evening and for the weekends. They come to this intensive program because their overall development is at risk: their health and growth are jeopardized and their peer and family relationships are compromised, with no sign that these profound effects can be reversed with outpatient management strategies. They are likely to have a co-existing condition, or conditions, like depression, anxiety, or OCD, which increase the challenges to their getting well.

The day hospital program model is based on milieu treatment strategies. Some aspects of it can be viewed as employing the model of gradual (hierarchical) and repeated exposure to feared situations, starting with the least feared situations. This is also known as "systematic desensitization" or "graduated exposure therapy" and is commonly used in the treatment of phobias, like the fear of heights (Tyron 2005). The common fears in eating disorders are weight gain and foods that are either associated with weight gain or with some other form of perceived harm. For some patients, suspending compensating behaviours like physical activity, vomiting, or laxative use, may be required simultaneously with the exposure therapy, because the fears of weight gain and various foods can only be faced when the compensation for the food intake is prevented. Other fears, like school-related and social fears, and their connections with the eating disorder, can be addressed in the day program because the interconnections are more easily observed in an all-day program that has school, peer group, and meal components.

The day hospital program uses a family-based treatment model (Lock *et al.* 2001). This treatment can be conducted separately or conjointly (Eisler 2005), meaning that parents and children may attend therapy sessions either separately or together. The day hospital program works separately with the teens and with parents, but brings them together weekly for individual family meetings and again for family education night. At family education night there is a joint program for parents and their children, followed by a support group for parents and a recreation hour for children. This weekly group is an important part of keeping parents motivated and educated so that their children will stay in the program until the family and/or the teen are able to manage without it.

The role of the psychiatrist

The psychiatrist, who is the director of the program, meets weekly or at least every two weeks with each teen. The purpose of these meetings is to understand the teens, support their motivation to get well, and to evaluate any co-morbid psychiatric illnesses. This includes the associated safety concerns of suicidal preoccupation or intent and any self-harm behaviours, because the high mortality in eating disorders is comprised in part by suicides. The psychiatrist may also evaluate the need for psycho-pharmaceutical medication, or the need to monitor any such medications already being taken.

The day hospital program is an ideal place for the psychiatrist to understand the teen. Through the psychiatrist's own meetings with the participants and with the daily observations of staff, the psychiatrist can develop an understanding of the psychological manifestations of the eating disorder at the micro-level: in school, groups, family, and the milieu. These observations help with formulating what is bringing the child back to the eating disorder over and over again, which provides the basis for a treatment plan. It is also an ideal environment in which to observe the effects of medications.

The program psychiatrist and a family worker generally co-facilitate family education night, although other program staff may step in from time to time.

The role of the family therapist

Several family therapists provide therapy for the families in the program. Each family is assigned to a specific therapist who holds weekly family therapy sessions with them. The goal of these meetings is the same as it is in outpatient family-based therapy: to help the parents increase their child's food intake as needed and to reduce or eliminate compensating behaviours as required (see Chapter 4). The program provides the child's food intake during the week, but every weekend the parents take back responsibility, and the family therapy sessions help them to prepare for this. Also, parents phone their family therapist every Monday to let the therapist know what went well and what did not. After weekly rounds, where all of the team members discuss each participant's progress, the therapist gives feedback to the parents about how their child is progressing. These conversations may establish issues that are dealt with at the weekly session – for instance, if the child is losing weight on the weekends.

The family therapist also meets with the family for re-entry meetings if these are needed. A re-entry meeting is held when a child refuses a part of the program: completing a meal or attending a group, for instance. This process is described in detail further along in this chapter.

Individual therapy is offered once a teen is established in the program and has engaged with the other group members. The exception to this would be a teen with severe social phobia who needs to learn some ways of managing in a group before being exposed to the challenge of eating meals in a peer-group setting. Some teens choose to use individual therapy once it is offered, and some do not. The family therapists also provide individual therapy.

The role of the dietitian

The physician and a dietitian together establish a "progress weight"[17] for each teen. The dietitian works out the corresponding meal requirements and supports the teens to choose menus. Liquid meal supplements are rarely used. The dietitian also helps structure opportunities for the participants to approach feared foods and co-facilitates a weekend planning group where participants set goals for the weekend meals, among other things. The dietitian provides education to participants and families about food intake, energy and nutritional needs, and how these are related to a person's activity pattern.

The role of the physician

In our day hospital program a physician monitors the medical wellbeing of participants. This requires a weekly physical examination when blood pressure and pulse are taken lying and standing, as well as lab work that includes a full blood picture or CBC, urea, electrolytes, electrocardiogram (ECG), and so on. Participants' weights are taken one to three times weekly, depending on whether they are weight-stable or still in a weight-gain or weight-stabilization phase. The physician may attend family therapy meetings from time to time to discuss medical test results or to answer parents' questions about their child's physical health. As required, the physician will meet with a teen to determine whether age-appropriate development is occurring or discuss any other health concerns.

---

17 A "progress weight" is the weight assessed by the team as the minimum required to support the teen's development and is revised as needed in the process of recovery, e.g. if a 14-year-old reaches her progress weight and in the process grows in height, her progress weight will be increased so as to support further growth in height. In other programs, how the goal weight is set depends on the lead or most responsible clinician.

The role of the child and youth counsellors

Child and youth counsellors (CYCs),[18] along with the rest of the team members, provide milieu support and lead some of the program groups. A CYC or a dietitian plus one of the other staff members are present at every meal and snack to provide supervision and to eat along with the participants. Each participant has a primary CYC. The CYC helps the participant develop and apply an individualized treatment plan in collaboration with her family and treatment team. The CYC also supports the participant to bring issues to group and family therapy.

CHILEAN MINERS AND THE RESCUE

Thirty-three miners in Chile were trapped 600 ft underground for two months after a collapse in the copper and gold mine where they worked. They were surviving in a 500-square-foot space. When the new tunnel needed for their rescue was finished, one of the rescuers rode through it in the rescue capsule first. Why? The rescuers wanted to test the capsule and show the miners that the tunnel was a safe and secure way for them to get out of the mine to their loved ones. Having survived in their harsh environment for so long, the miners were worried about the risks of trying for something better.

In the day hospital program, the staff members go down onto the raft (see "The leaky raft" on p.80) with the teens. Every staff member in the program eats at least one meal with the participants every week. The teens are frightened about what it will be like to get well and they benefit from the reassurance that it is safe.

CYCs also lead the food desensitization group. In the group teens are encouraged to face feared situations that may contribute to the maintenance of their eating disorders. The group may involve eating a meal or snack that has been difficult or avoided, for example a buffet at a restaurant, a movie with typical movie snacks, or baking cookies in the program kitchen and eating them. At other times it will involve

---

18 The primary role of the CYCs is to support the teens through the challenges of the program. In other places, child life support workers or child and youth workers may fulfill this role.

facing body image issues by going shopping for clothing at the mall or going to the beach and wearing swimwear.

The role of the teacher

There is a qualified teacher and classroom available in the day program where students continue to accumulate credits toward their high-school diplomas. While in the program, the teens attend school for several hours each day. The teacher maintains communication with the student's home school so that transition to and from program happens effectively, and plans the student's program jointly with her and her parents. Initially some parents may hesitate, thinking that their child's school record will show that she has been in hospital. This does not happen. The teacher is part of the regular school board and all the student's marks and credits appear together on the school record as they normally would.

The role of weekly rounds

Every week the whole team meets to bring together their observations and experiences of each of the participants in the program and to plan the next step in treatment, based on the most complete information possible. This meeting enables the staff to be "on the same page" with these plans, which is essential to the care of the participants. Students who are doing their placements or rotations in the day hospital enjoy this part of the program as it is an excellent opportunity to experience interprofessional practice.

Recent research has shown that the average length of stay in our day program for those with anorexia and no co-morbid disorders is about six months (Boachie, Girz and LaFrance 2010; Grewal *et al.* 2011). Those patients with bulimia who need symptom interruption and are stabilizing their weight may need less time in the program. Patients with anorexia or bulimia who have complicating factors like major depressive disorder or an anxiety disorder (including OCD) usually need more time. This is consistent with Lock *et al.* (2005) whose research with outpatient therapy found that teens with OCD-like eating disorder behaviours or those living in single parent families tend to need more time.

The decision to attend the day program

Parents can be reluctant to make the commitment to bringing their child to the day program because it interrupts schooling. School may be the only area in which their child has been able to continue performing at a high level and this may create the illusion that she is not too ill. To interrupt schooling in this context looks like a substantial and uncertain risk. Parents can underestimate the danger of the eating disorder, unaware that their child has sacrificed everything else to maintain school performance. Food restriction and bingeing and purging make concentration difficult, and projects that could previously be done in one hour can take several hours to complete. The methods their child is using to manage her schooling are not sustainable and, if left unaddressed, can result in a big school interruption later.

LOW INTEREST RATES AND THE LONG-TERM MORTGAGE

You sign on to a mortgage for your house when the interest rates are very low. It is a big mortgage and will take you 15 to 20 years to pay off. Your salary is just enough to cover the mortgage and other expenses, with a little left over for recreation.

Things go along fine for several years and then the interest rates start creeping up. You put your recreation funds into your mortgage account. Your employer hits hard times and you do not get a raise. The mortgage rates keep going up and you cannot pay. If you can't find a way to pay, you lose your house.

Similarly, with an eating disorder, your child is using every bit of energy she has to keep up with school, but as she gets into the higher grades, the demands increase. When they become more than she can manage, she may either leave school in a crisis, or fail and lose her confidence.

Taking this extra time in high school will not significantly affect future education and career in the way that dropping out of university later would affect them. However, the child's own fears about coming to the program may be expressed as anxiety about losing time at school.

It is as though the child is asking, "Is it really so important for me to come here that I should miss time at school? How important is it to you, Mom and Dad, that I do this fearful thing? Are you sure this is the right thing to do?" As described in the "Treasures and Traps" activity in Chapter 5, the teens want their parents to take the lead because they cannot take the decision themselves. (See also "The 911 call" on p.17.)

The question of whether the day hospital program is the right place to be comes up frequently for the teens, especially in the first four to eight weeks of the program, and intermittently after that. The teens need their parents to help them stay in the program when they feel like running away, and in order to support them, parents need to be sure it is right to keep them there. For this they need to have a full appreciation of the way eating disorders work and of how the program works. Parents play a vital and essential role during treatment and continue to play a significant role after treatment.

Meal supervision

Up to eight teens between the ages of 13 and 18 attend the program five days per week and have all of their meals and snacks there in a group with their peers, supervised by staff. This helps to stop the deterioration of their health and they can begin the process of recovery. In this way the program temporarily takes over for the parents and gives them a break from the unrelenting struggle of managing the eating disorder symptoms on a daily basis. When a teen enters the program and starts eating, it may appear to parents that it is easy for staff to get their child to eat and then they feel guilty about having had such difficulty with this task themselves. However, it is not the parents' fault. Several factors contribute to making it happen and they are not available in a family setting. One is that staff time is not limited, while parent time is limited. Two staff members, including at least one CYC and/or a dietitian, are present at every meal and there is nothing else that requires their attention besides supporting the participants to eat their meals. While delaying eating at home might result in an emotional upset that ends with parents having to go to work and the meal remaining uneaten, delaying eating in the program results in concerted efforts to prevent this from recurring and to ensure that all the food needed by the participant is finally eaten.

The program harnesses several dynamics to help the teens complete their meals in a timely way: staff guidance, structure, peer support, and parental encouragement. An experienced dietitian helps prepare teens to eat in the program by involving them in planning their meals and choosing their food, and introduces challenging foods in a gradual and hierarchical way (starting with the least difficult foods). On the other hand, the amount of food required is determined by the dietitian and is rarely negotiable. The program does not compromise in this area because the child's development is at stake (see Chapter 3). CYCs introduce the teen to the dining-room rules and enforce these rules at mealtimes if needed. For example, teens are not permitted to cut foods into small pieces or to crumble foods, because these behaviours are usually associated with hiding food, and all food containers must be completely cleared of food, otherwise the participant will feel the need to test how much food can be left uneaten before staff say it is too much. The rules are designed to limit eating disorder behaviours and to relieve teens from the pressure to compete to be the best at having an eating disorder. They make it safer to eat. At the table, however, the teens may feel angry with the staff for watching them and say, "Quit staring at me!" Their impulses to hide or otherwise lose food make them feel criticized and judged by the observing staff. If the staff members happen to stop watching them, though, they feel overwhelmed at being left alone with these impulses at a table where other teens may be acting on similar ones.

Because teens start and end the program at individually determined times, there are always some teens in the program who are more "senior" and have a more established pro-recovery mindset than more recently arrived teens. The peer group has an important role in the recovery of participants. Peers gently support newcomers to complete their meals by empathizing with the difficulties of getting started in the program and letting the new teen know that it gets easier as time goes on. They share coping strategies that have helped them, from conversational distraction and calming, to encouragements like "You can do it," or actually going bite for bite when a food is experienced as very difficult. Or they may make recommendations like "Just hold your nose and finish." Teens can more easily trust and accept support that comes from other teens who also have eating disorders and are eating similar amounts of food, than they can trust support from staff, even though the staff eat along with them.

WHEN A STATEMENT IS ACTUALLY A QUESTION

Daughter: Mom, I'm going to a party at Christine's house on Friday.

Mom: Where will her parents be?

Daughter: They are out of town.

Mom: Who will be there?

Daughter: Just our friends and Christine's older brother.

Mom: Isn't he the one who bought alcohol for Christine last time?

Daughter: Yes, but he isn't going to do that this time.

Mom: Just the same, sweetheart, you are not going to go to the party. We have said before "no parents, no party."

The daughter in this story is telling her mother she is going to a party, but at another level she is asking her mother to make the decision for her not to go. Unlike teens in many situations, she is being honest with her mother about the facts of the party. She does not want her friends to think she is a "loser," but she is also afraid of being in a situation where she and her friends, acting on impulse, may end up in a very risky situation. If her mother makes the decision, she is prevented from attending but she saves face with her friends.

Participants are also kept accountable to the group when they do not complete a meal or do not complete a meal on time. Because these are eating disorder behaviours, they have the effect of triggering all the members of the group, who themselves will then feel less like finishing the next meal or snack on time, or at all. So time is taken to "process," that is, to discuss in the group any delays in completing or not completing meals or snacks: how these have affected the group members, how those who finished on time managed to do so, and what each member can do to prevent a recurrence. Using this "existing expertise" is not unique to a day hospital program.

FIRST TIME TO THE WORLD CUP

When a soccer team gets to the finals in the World Cup for the first time, there are many challenges to face: the enormous audience, the huge stakes, highly talented competitors, and insecurities that emerge in the new context. If some members of the team have been to the World Cup before, they can guide the others on how to step up to meet these challenges, and how to stay calmer and focused in the face of them.

Parents may worry that in a day program their child will be exposed to more eating disordered behaviours, new "tricks of the trade" which will make things worse. Under the supervision of staff, this will happen only in limited ways. If you were taking your team to the World Cup, would you rather start with all new players or with some who have senior knowledge and experience?

Re-entry meetings

If, after all of the staff and peer support and time devoted to helping a teen complete her meal, she does not complete it, she is required to leave the program temporarily. This ensures a safe environment for eating for the other group members. Her family worker/therapist then arranges a family re-entry meeting as soon as possible: either on the same day or before breakfast the next day. This ensures the greatest possible continuity of sufficient nutrition for the teen who did not complete her meal, and indicates how crucial it is that she eat all of the food that is prescribed.

When the teen leaves the program under these circumstances, it is likely that she believes she is being given too much food, and is experiencing a strong urge to get away from the program. Once she is home, she may initially feel relieved to be away from the food, but then guilty that she has caused her parents the inconvenience of leaving work to pick her up and to attend the re-entry meeting. She will also be wondering again whether she is really meant to eat as much food as is served to her at the program. It is possible that she will express these feelings to her parents by saying things like how stupid the program is, how picky and mean the staff are, and how she is expected to eat so much that she always has a stomach-ache. If her parents agree with her and then take her back to the program, it will be difficult for her to stay there.

THE BABYSITTER

Suppose you bring your children home from the babysitter's and they complain about what the babysitter is like. If you listen to them and then say that the babysitter is stupid or mean, it will be a problem the next morning if you start packing up their things and say "Ready now? It's time to go to the babysitter's." If the babysitter is a good one, then it may be that your child is just being asked to do things somewhat differently from the way they are done at home. Or maybe she refused and the babysitter gave her consequences for this. Your child wants to know whether you agree that she should do as the babysitter asks.

Young people with eating disorders suffer many doubts throughout the process of recovery, and they may raise these doubts indirectly as very assertive or even aggressive statements rather than directly through calm questions. If you maintain your balance in the face of these challenging statements and affirm your child's need to have all of her nutrition without compensations like exercise or purging, she will find it easier to eat.

The family re-entry meeting is designed to help everyone involved to be on the same page. Eating disorders thrive on divisions between people, so it is important to dissolve any barriers that prevent staff and parents/caregivers from acting together to support the teen. Events leading up to the staff decision to send the teen home are reviewed. The teen is given the first opportunity to tell what happened. Her CYC will be in attendance and will support her to express her feelings. The CYC will also offer alternative explanations for why the teen may have refused the meal. For example, the teen may have believed she'd been sitting for too long or eaten too much earlier in the day and could not believe she could continue to sit or to eat more without immediately becoming fat. The CYC may also discuss features of the day that she thinks may have contributed to the difficulties. Parents are invited to ask questions and to express any concerns they have about the way things are done in the program. The family therapist and CYC will answer these concerns until they are settled. Sometimes issues are raised by the teen or parents that need to be followed up by staff in the program – for example, a teen's view that a staff member has implemented rules unfairly, or a conflict arising between peers.

When there are no issues remaining, parents will let their child know that she is expected to continue in the program and follow the program protocols. The teen is then asked to re-affirm that she will follow these protocols, and is brought back into the program. Any nutrition that she needs to make up as a result of having been out of the program is discussed with parents present, and the CYC arranges for the nutrition to be added to the day's meals or snacks in a way that is manageable.

PAYING OFF A CREDIT CARD

Imagine there are two girls. They each have a credit card with $1000 credit available. They both go shopping. One of them pays the total she's charged to the card every month one day before the due date. The other pays the total she's charged to the card every month, but she pays it one day after the due date. Which one will still owe a lot of money at the end of the year?

It does not get easier for a child with an eating disorder to eat something "later." Putting off or avoiding nutrition during the day usually reinforces the restriction and becomes a means to not eating the food at all.

Family re-entry meetings may be needed at other times to engage parental support in helping a participant to change a behaviour and to stay in the program. Significant instances of a teen not following staff directives or program protocols can result in the teen being sent home, with the re-entry meeting being scheduled very soon afterwards. Examples include: refusing to attend a group, verbally abusing or demeaning staff or other participants, and using excluded substances like caffeine or laxatives in the program. If these behaviours are left unchallenged, participants who are following directives and protocols will feel they are being needlessly compliant, and the program's pro-recovery culture will be undermined.

In the re-entry meeting we follow the same structure as in re-entry meetings for incomplete meals. If necessary, the family worker explains the rationale for the protocol to the participant and the parents, and so they understand why we take the situation very seriously and have interrupted at least one parent's workday to deal with it. Sometimes teens will challenge protocols as a way of trying to get "kicked out" so that they don't have to continue with treatment. Parents can help them stay in treatment when they are not yet motivated to do so themselves. This is a great advantage that is not available to adults seeking treatment. In adult treatment programs, although the staff work very hard to increase participants' motivation, they are often less successful because participants are dealing directly with the illness without support from anyone else. In this context recovery depends on the participants' own motivations and eating disorders are a-motivational illnesses.

CASE EXAMPLE: EMMA

Emma started the program after having been an inpatient for three months. Like her family, she enjoys sports. Her eating disorder developed when she restricted her food intake and increased her physical activity levels. She found it very difficult to tolerate being on bed rest while she was an inpatient and was often found exercising in her room. Her treatment team referred her directly to the day hospital program because the risk of relapse is very high for those who exercise excessively (Carter et al. 2004). At meals, she frequently gets up unnecessarily "to get something," completes her food very quickly, and then urges other teens to hurry up. She may delay going to the classroom or to a group and may stand in the hall or another room instead. When walking from one part of program to another, she always takes the longest route possible. When in the classroom or a group, she finds it difficult to sit still and may sit restlessly on the edge of her chair, or repeatedly find reasons to get up again. She finds it very difficult to stop these behaviours even when asked to, and even if she knows she will have to eat more to make up for what she loses through the activity. On some days she may feel the staff are asking for too much and will push the limits.

As with other aspects of the program, if Emma or any other participant refuses to follow staff directives or to take part in required parts of the program, this becomes what is known as a "program refusal" and she will need to have a family re-entry meeting. While she waits for her family to arrive, the rule is that a participant must sit outside the program area (with staff present). On this day, Emma had delayed many times and was outright refusing to go to the group room where everyone was waiting to start Group Dynamics. Finally she was told that she would need to have a re-entry meeting. As one member of staff tried to escort her to the waiting area and another went to call her parents, Emma calmly said she was glad to have an excuse to leave, and left the hospital.

After a couple of hours Emma returned to the hospital accompanied by her parents, who had been called by staff to let them know what happened and to ask them to bring Emma back to hospital as soon as possible for a re-entry. Emma was telling them about the "crazy" program rules while they waited for her family worker and CYC to begin the re-entry meeting. Emma did not want to sit down for the meeting, as she was hoping to delay sitting as long as possible. However, her mom and dad insisted that she sit for the meeting, as that had been agreed on the week before. Emma sat on the edge of her chair and told everyone to get on with it.

The family worker first asked the CYC to talk about what had gone well with Emma over the past couple of days and the CYC described how Emma had succeeded in following staff directives about sitting most of the time, even though she was clearly feeling frequent strong urges to get up and move around. Emma was then asked to tell what might have made things more difficult today. She said that she is not sick like the other girls in program who don't like to eat and that she does not belong in the program – it has nothing to offer her. As the staff and family discussed this with Emma, her CYC mentioned that some of the girls at breakfast had reacted to Emma's rushing them to finish and told her to relax. Also, she had eaten a hot breakfast that included pancakes and syrup, which might have triggered some intense urges to become active. Emma denied that the pancakes bothered her and said that she often eats them for brunch on weekends after going for a long run. She looked at her parents for agreement, as she said that everyone in her family likes to eat and to be active. Emma's parents agreed, but pointed out that Emma has taken this to the extreme, which has caused cardiac complications, and that she needs to learn to be more moderate.

It was decided in the meeting that the staff would work out a gentle but steady process for Emma to increase her sitting times in the classroom, at meals, and in groups. Emma's parents encouraged her to use staff support to work out her issues with the other participants, starting with telling them about her challenges with sitting.

Then Emma's parents asked if it would be okay for Emma to play soccer or baseball in the evenings after program. They felt that she would find it easier to sit during program hours if she knew she could be active in the evenings. Also, they felt this would be more "normal." Even kids at school who sit all day are often very active in the evening. Emma was very positive about this idea. The family worker explained, however, that this would not be a good idea at this time. It would reinforce the eating disorder's rule that any food eaten must be compensated for and more. Giving Emma vigorous physical activity time to help her accept her body's need to have rest would prevent this healing. The eating disorder is like a fracture and needs more time to heal.

THE FRACTURED BONE

A young woman injures her ankle while doing gymnastics. At first it appears to be a simple sprain, but turns out to be a fracture. On the surface it looks healed, but it is actually in need of continued rest to complete the healing.

A family who understands sports also understands fractures. In their estimation a sprain does not take long to heal, and possibly they see the cardiac problem as a fracture, but the eating disorder as a sprain. Their child is most vulnerable at this stage, so if they let her play now she is likely to hurt herself. She will be able to play at a later time.

Like many parents who are learning to appreciate the complex ways an eating disorder works, Emma's parents are unintentionally advocating for the eating disorder in an effort to relieve their daughter of distress. Unfortunately, this way of relieving distress is like getting rid of a bully by giving him what he demands. He will come back for more. Instead, Emma's parents can reassure her that she needs to rest, to heal, and to be nourished. When she has fully healed, there will be time to engage in physical activities that are for pleasure and social fun.

Family education night

One night per week, all of the parents attend an evening program that has two parts. The first hour holds an activity that parents and children participate in together. It might be one of the activities described in the section on multi-family group therapy (see Chapter 5) that brings out the issue of trust in recovery, allows exchanging of multiple perspectives, or encourages problem-solving together. After the activity is debriefed in the large group, the children leave for a recreational hour while the parents have a parent support group facilitated by a staff member.

In the support group, parents who are further along in the treatment process lend their expertise to newer members of the group. Senior parents tell stories about how they managed the weekends, which helps newer parents understand how to handle meals and post-meal supervision, what to expect, and how to be authoritative without being authoritarian or abusive. Weekends early in the treatment process can be especially challenging because of efforts on the part of the children to lose any weight that they gained during the program week.

A few times a year, a friends and siblings night is held, so that friends and siblings can learn more about eating disorders. Siblings are encouraged to attend family meetings, but are often unable to attend regularly due to school, or they may prefer not to. Once a month the activity in the first hour of family education night is "family meals." Parents bring food that has been agreed on at the previous week's meeting. All the families sit together, with staff sitting nearby, and everyone eats dinner together. How could one meal in a month make any difference?

SAILING OFF THE EDGE OF THE WORLD

In medieval Europe most people thought that the world was flat. No one wanted to sail far across the ocean because they believed their ships would fall over the edge of the world and they would die. When people learned that the world is round, they could sail and sail away without fearing the end of the world.

Young people with eating disorders have convinced their parents that they are unable to eat many foods. Parents stop expecting their children to eat foods outside of this tiny comfort zone. At family meals night parents see that their children can eat a wide variety of foods with no ill effects: the avoidance was based on misinformation and fear, not on reality. With this shift in perspective, parents know it is safe for them to support their children to eat a wider variety of foods at home.

Parents of children with eating disorders have been used to understanding their children's rejection of different foods as based on something rational, for example they are unable to digest the food; or they have accepted that their children find the foods disgusting or gross, and so have stopped expecting that they will eat them. In the program avoided foods, with very few exceptions, are gradually re-introduced into meals and snacks. At "family meals" parents see their children eat a full meal or a specific food for the first time in years.

They see that their children can do this without undue stress, helped by the support of their peers. After the meal is over, parents hear some of the more senior teens talk about having gone through this process earlier and how now they enjoy many of the foods that they previously avoided.

Reaching progress weight

The participants in our program are not shown their weight and are not told what their goal weight or progress weight is. Parents are also strongly encouraged not to keep scales in their homes. It is our experience that it is more helpful to provide the teens with a space where they do not have to focus on numbers. After all, there are weigh scales nearly everywhere – it is not esoteric information that is being kept from them. Because the program is a "numbers-free zone," participants get through all of the meals and snacks of the day without checking the minute-by-minute impact on their weight. When they don't have the numbers to focus on, they learn, with the help of staff and peers, to manage the challenges of school, groups, and family sessions in more constructive ways. As they mobilize and develop the resources to better handle interpersonal situations and academic challenges, their self-esteem increases. Once they are feeling more effective in the world and stronger in themselves, the number associated with their weight takes on less importance.

We do not tell parents the progress weights either. Generally, it seems that if parents know the weights, their children will find a way to get the information. Most parents are comfortable with not knowing. However, sometimes parents feel invested in having their child leave the program at a weight that they feel is right, but which is not consistent with the pediatrician and dietitian's assessment. If the team believes that the child is not well enough to leave, then if the parents take the child out of the program anyway, the leaving will not be glorified with a "graduation certificate." Participants graduate from the program when they and their parents have completed all aspects of the program and there is consensus among staff that they can sustain this progress outside of the program.

TO TELL OR NOT TO TELL

You are reading a "thriller" and are very worried about what will happen to the lead character. Your older sister offers to tell you what happens in the end. Should you let her tell you? If you find out what happens it may relieve your worries, but on the other hand it may make it difficult for you to finish the story.

Young people in treatment for eating disorders may think that knowing their progress weight (goal weight) will make them less worried. If they hear it while weight means everything to them, it may stop them from continuing their work. Then they may never get to a place where their understanding changes so that numbers have far less significance for them.

Sometimes a child leaves the day hospital program without graduating. She may have gained enough weight to keep her safe from medical risk and may have sustained this weight for some time, but indicates consistently that she is not willing or ready to do the emotional and interpersonal work that would help insulate her from relapse. Her parents may not be willing to support her to stay and do this work. In this situation we do not hold our usual "graduation ceremony" when she leaves. We explain this to the family by saying that it is like graduating from high school, and if we were to give a diploma to the person who is a few credits short of the diploma requirements, we would be telling her that she is done while setting her up for relapse later.

HIGH-SCHOOL CREDITS

When you are close to finishing high school, you have to complete all your coursework and write the final exams. If an exam is not written or a course is otherwise not finished, you will not have the credits you need to graduate. Even though you feel you have finished to your own satisfaction, you will not get a high-school diploma. When you apply for university, you will not get in and will have to come back to high school to complete your requirements.

Group therapy

A major component of the day hospital program is group therapy, where participants meet with peers and two staff members to work together to learn new skills and coping strategies, challenge one another to complete goals and deal with fears, learn to deal with body image dissatisfaction and how to process interpersonal issues, and foster a sense of personal effectiveness. It is characteristic of young people who develop eating disorders that they are generous in helping others and reluctant to accept help. They often think that needing help shows there is "something wrong" with them and feel weak and ashamed for needing help. They may believe that for one reason or another their parents cannot help them or should not be bothered with their needs, and will hide their feelings and needs so that others are not required to help them. They convince themselves that they can manage on their own, always giving to others, and not relying on others to give to them. This isn't a sustainable practice. At some point they "run out of gas." (See "Driving with no gas" on p.62 and Figure 6.1 on the following page.)

In groups in the day hospital program, the participants learn to challenge this practice and the idea that they should be perfect. They are encouraged to identify their feelings and emotions and to express them, so that they can accept them and learn ways of coping and responding to situations that may be triggers. They also learn how to address interpersonal issues so as to develop constructive ways of solving problems in relationships. Learning these skills and developing confidence through them may be helpful for preventing relapse.

Being in a group can help reduce isolation and shame and can encourage the motivation needed to work at difficult issues. Seeing more senior participants simultaneously developing confidence and tolerating weight gain is very encouraging to newer participants.

Figure 6.1: The Good Samaritan
Drawing by Nadia Boachie 2010

Medication

Nutritional rehabilitation and psychotherapy (family, group, and individual) remain the primary interventions for children and adolescents with eating disorders. Psycho-pharmacological interventions are at best adjunct treatments for anorexia nervosa. In the research with adults SSRIs, particularly Prozac (fluoxetine), have been found helpful in the management of bulimia, against the urge to binge and purge, independent of depression or anxiety, especially in combination with cognitive-behavioural therapy.

These medications have side effects that can affect organs and systems that are already affected by the eating disorder: heart, liver, gastro-intestinal system, and hormonal system. Since there is very little research on the use of psycho-pharmacological medications with children or teens, each situation must be evaluated individually to determine whether the potential benefit of using them outweighs the risk of not trying them at all.

There are no medications that directly help those with anorexia to eat. However, it is common for anorexia to co-exist with depression, anxiety, and OCD, and these conditions complicate the recovery process. Medications can be considered as one component of treating these co-existing conditions.

Depression can be treated with the SSRIs, of which Prozac (fluoxetine) is approved for use with children and adolescents. Other SSRIs are sometimes prescribed to children or adolescents "off label," which means that the primary research has not usually been conducted with children and the effects are extrapolated from studies with adults. However, depression is also an effect of starvation, and until the starvation has been dealt with, it may not be possible to assess accurately whether the depression is induced by starvation or is a separately occurring disorder, unless there is an antecedent history of depression or a family history of depression. Some researchers have found that in those who are significantly underweight, SSRIs appear not to be as effective as when taken by those whose weight is normalized (Kaye *et al.* 2001). Because of these issues it makes clinical sense, when treating depression in children and adolescents with anorexia nervosa, to use these medications after weight restoration.

Even then teens and/or their parents may be very reluctant to try a medication. Sometimes this is because of general principles about relying on medication rather than "relying on oneself," or because a medication may be the same as one being taken by another family member for a different mental illness. There are many concerns and also myths about medication. Many conversations may be needed to clear up the myths.

TENNIS SHOES, SOCCER BOOTS, AND MEDICATION

Venus Williams and David Beckham are exceptionally talented athletes: Williams is well known for her tennis skills and Beckham for soccer. What would happen if Williams and Beckham had to play their sports wearing bedroom slippers instead of their well-designed tennis shoes and soccer boots? They would certainly not play as well. Even a champion cannot show the full range and level of her or his talents without excellent footwear.

People can have strong feelings against taking medication and may not take it regularly even if it is prescribed. Medications don't give you talents you don't have or take away talents you do have. Just as well-designed footwear aids the athlete, medication can make some things easier for people – for example, it can make decision-making easier, so that they can move from decisions to actions and fully express their talents.

TRAFFIC LIGHTS AND THE PERSON WITH OCD

If you have OCD, there are so many things you are thinking about that you have difficulty sorting anything out. It's like going through an intersection where the traffic lights aren't working: things go very slowly, there is confusion, and there can be collisions. If a policeman comes and directs traffic, it makes driving through the intersection easier.

Does that mean the policeman is driving for you? No.

It is similar with medication: you will still be making all the decisions and determining your life. The medication is taking away overwhelming distractions so that your mind is clear and you can decide which turns to take and which roads to drive along.

Day hospital programs for children and adolescents have been operating in Canada for more than ten years. We have found them very helpful clinically and they help most young people who attend them. We are currently studying them to tease out which components contribute the most to their success. They fill a gap for many adolescents with eating disorders who need more structure than weekly outpatient therapy but do not need a medical intervention like an inpatient unit. Over their time in the day program, parents can experience how their children's eating disorders can be dealt with physically and psychologically. Then, when their children become outpatients, following graduation from the day program, parents are better prepared to continue helping with their children's recovery. This helps to avoid repeated re-admissions to inpatient units, which are usually associated with poor long-term outcome.

Chapter 7

Inpatient Treatment

When a child or teen with an eating disorder, especially anorexia nervosa, is admitted to hospital for inpatient treatment, it is usually because there is a medical or psychiatric crisis. A medical crisis can arise from restriction of food and liquid intake; from compensatory behaviours like exercising, purging, or laxative use; or from a combination of both. Features that carry increased medical risk include:

- exercise with low weight

- vomiting with blood

- poor fluid intake with poor nutrition

- rapid weight loss

- acute starvation

- laxative use.

A hospital admission must be considered when any of the following characteristics are present on physical examination or in blood work, as they may indicate medical risk:

- weight < 85 percent or BMI < 17.5 kg/m² (problems with BMI)[19]

- heart rate (HR) near 40 beats per minute (bpm) (HR < 50 bpm daytime; < 45 bpm at night)

- orthostatic hypotension with an increase in pulse rate of > 20 bpm (at the Hospital for Sick Children in Toronto this has to be > 35 bpm for inpatient admission)

- blood pressure (BP) of > 10-20 mm Hg/min[20] drop from supine to standing

- BP < 80/50 mm Hg

- hypokalemia (insufficient potassium), 3mmol/l,[21] hypophosphatemia (insufficient phosphate) < 0.5 mmol/l, hypomagnesemia (insufficient magnesium) < 0.5 mmol/l

- QTc[22] prolongation from ECG.

While each of these is a powerful measure, generally a combination would be considered for admission (American Psychiatric Association 2006).

There are also psychiatric indications for admission, which include acute food refusal, uncontrollable bingeing and purging, acute psychiatric emergencies such as suicidal ideation, or the presence of a co-morbid diagnosis.

A significant proportion of young people with eating disorders have co-existing conditions, most commonly depression, OCD, and anxiety disorders. Depression may be pre-existing or a consequence of starvation and social isolation. Co-existing conditions may be treated simultaneously with the eating disorder, so long as the child or teen is medically stable and not in an acute starvation state.

---

19 BMI is an indicator that further examination should be made, but it is not reliable as a single measure especially when used with children or adolescents.

20 Millimetres of mercury per minute.

21 Millimoles per litre.

22 An interval measured by the ECG.

CASE EXAMPLE: SONYA

Sonya is a 16-year-old girl who had been repeatedly bullied and harassed about her body weight at school. After her sister went on a diet and lost some weight, Sonya decided to try the diet plus exercising and lost over 50 percent of her body weight in six months. Her family doctor referred her for an eating disorder assessment. When she arrived for the assessment, she was examined by a pediatrician and was found to have a very low heart rate (bradycardia) and very low blood pressure (hypotension). She had fainted at school twice in the previous two weeks. The pediatrician also noticed that Sonya had fine lanugo hair on her face, back, arms, and legs. Sonya had difficulty concentrating during the assessment, and her mother completed the answers to several of the questions the assessment team asked. Following the assessment, Sonya and her family were advised by the assessment team to accept an admission to the inpatient unit, which they did.

After admission, a team consisting of a pediatrician, a psychiatrist, a dietitian, a nurse, and a family therapist is assigned to the family. They meet and decide on what Sonya's goal weight will be and how much weight they will expect her to gain per week. These expectations are specific to individual patients and to the stage of the inpatient stay. Sonya will be put on full bedrest with a heart monitor. If she is found out of bed without staff permission, she may be moved to a room where she can be constantly observed because of her slowed heart rate (bradycardia) and the possibility of having a fainting episode due to postural hypotension (see "The half-full bottle" on p.61 and "The television remote control" on p.59). Other occasions when a patient could be moved to constant observation include when there is a risk of self-harm or suicide.

One of the most significant concerns of the pediatrician and dietitian will be to avoid the potential problem referred to as "re-feeding syndrome" as they begin the process of re-nourishing Sonya. This usually occurs if heart rate has been seriously slowed as a result of massive weight loss, when the sudden introduction of carbohydrates may force the heart to beat faster than it should; this could trigger a very fast paced heart rhythm, referred to as Torsades arrhythmia (see "The fluorescent light and the incandescent light" on p.62). This can be very confounding to parents, who want nothing more than to have their child fed well and then hear that care must be taken with carbohydrate quantity. They may be surprised by the caution applied to feeding, but there is a real danger of death, especially in the first few weeks, due to starvation-related depletion of phosphate, magnesium, and potassium. When carbohydrate metabolism increases dramatically after a period of starvation, the insulin that is released causes a shift of these minerals from outside the cells to inside the cells. The sudden drop in the levels outside the cells can cause cardiac, respiratory, and/or circulatory system failures. To prevent this, the dietitian makes the menus low in carbohydrates, while the pediatrician monitors phosphate, magnesium, and potassium levels regularly and prescribes an appropriate mineral supplement (see "The factory and the recession" on p.65).

Once a week the team will meet with Sonya and her parents to review her progress since the previous week. They will discuss her progress with weight gain (though not in specific terms), daytime and nighttime heart rates, blood pressure, temperature, ECG, weight, and pertinent blood work, which may include full blood count, electrolytes (potassium, sodium, chloride, etc.), blood urea and nitrogen, creatinine, glucose, calcium, magnesium, and phosphorus. They will make recommendations about Sonya's care for the following week, including whether she needs more food, needs to continue on bedrest or to wear the heart monitor all the time or only at night, whether she can use the washroom on her own, and later whether she can have a pass to leave the hospital for a few hours or go home overnight. The family can ask questions and make requests at this time also.

As the risk of re-feeding syndrome recedes, attention can be turned to helping Sonya to gain weight. During this period, as the child's gastro-intestinal system recovers from persistent starvation, it is likely she will experience nausea, bloating, and/or stomach-aches after eating. Unless there are other causes, this is not dangerous and is simply due to delayed gastric emptying (see "The stomach is a muscle" on p.82). Usually these problems are resolved through regular food intake, although in some situations, doctors may recommend the use of a high fibre supplement. For the greatest part of the inpatient stay, there will be a nurse present whenever Sonya is eating a meal or snack. The nurse in this role will keep the conversation light and general and will watch for hiding of food. Sonya will be expected to consume all of her food within a specific time frame, so that she does not fall behind. The team will discuss logical consequences if Sonya is not able to follow these expectations or if she refuses food. For instance, some patients find it easier to use a liquid meal supplement to start with or for part of some meals. Sonya will also be weighed each morning before breakfast wearing a hospital gown and underwear. As in the day hospital program, she will not be informed of her weight. The nurse or dietitian who weighs her will watch that she is not hiding items on her body or in any other way falsifying her weight. If the team suspects deception in this area, they may take her weight at random times.

The key part of the admission is to restore Sonya's weight as close as possible to her progress weight[23] at a rate that is not overwhelming, but as quickly as possible. After a few weeks of inpatient treatment the child's condition stabilizes, she is eating without argument under the nurse's supervision, and

---

23 Research has shown that the closer the patient's weight is to a healthy weight when leaving hospital, the less likely it is that there will be a need for another admission (Baran, Weltzin and Kaye 1995; Rome *et al.* 2003).

the sense of crisis subsides. The admission usually allows the parents and team to work collaboratively to achieve maximum help for their child in a short time and to give the family a foothold on their child's recovery.

IF SHE IS STABLE, WHY CAN'T I TAKE HER HOME?

A parent asks: "The physician says that my child's vitals are stable. Doesn't that mean that she is okay and I can take her home?"

Answer: Being stable does not mean being well. Imagine a famous actress has been in a terrible car accident and is rushed to hospital. The next day on the news you hear that she is in stable condition. This does not mean she is well enough to leave hospital. It means that currently there is no major fluctuation in her vital signs and it is expected that she will live.

As the parents' anxiety decreases, their child's anxiety will likely increase. The child is aware that her parents are taking time away from work and from her siblings to be with her at hospital and to attend team meetings. They may be driving long distances. While in hospital she has "abandoned" her role as star student or family helper, and has not been able to work at her job. She feels responsible and guilty for these things.

BIG TRASH CANS AND LITTLE TRASH CANS

Young people with eating disorders are always taking care of others, suppressing their own needs. They try to rescue their parents and avoid burdening them with their emotions.

Emotions are essential to human life. But some emotions may be harmful to children who don't know what to do with them and are afraid their parents won't be able to handle them. These emotions have to be expressed – it's like emptying the trash can. It has to be emptied or it will overflow. Young people have "little trash cans," which will quickly fill up and overflow. They need to know that their parents have "big trash cans" and can take a lot.

Sonya will also have begun to gain weight, which in this context may translate for her as becoming fat and lazy. It is likely that she will start agitating for her parents to take her out of hospital. She may tell them that she understands now that she needs to eat and promises that she will eat on her own at home.

It is the most natural thing in the world for parents to believe their child when she says this. However, recognizing the effects of the illness does not translate directly into the ability to change it.

CHANGING THE ECONOMY

In an economic recession, award-winning economists may come to understand what's wrong with the economy and how it should be, but they don't know how to make the changes happen.

Through an inpatient admission, a child with an eating disorder may recognize the real effects of the eating disorder, but this doesn't mean that she can do things on her own to change it.

There is a much better chance of Sonya doing well if she stays in hospital long enough to recover most of the weight that she needs for optimal physical and emotional growth and development. For this to happen she needs to continue to eat frequently and to rest nearly all the time. As Sonya's energy begins to return, she may complain to her parents that she is tired of being stuck in bed in a room where she is getting fat and is not allowed to exercise. She may point out that she can't go to school and is falling behind her peers. Parents may then get angry with the staff for being "unreasonable" – for keeping Sonya at rest for so long while she continues to gain weight. It may seem unreasonable, but in fact it is necessary.

WHY DOES SHE HAVE TO EAT SO MUCH? WHY CAN'T SHE EXERCISE?

When a baby is born, she does little more than eat and sleep and will almost double in weight in the first five months. By the end of the first year, she will have tripled her birth weight. This intensive eating and sleeping is necessary for the baby to develop normally. Between one and two years of age, the child will gain very little weight – only about two more kilograms – because she is very active learning to walk, which takes a lot of energy because it involves exercise and defying gravity. Later on the rate of weight gain slows down or speeds up – depending on the stage of development the child or teen is at.

For a parent, having a teen who is recovering from an eating disorder is like nourishing an infant again – in fact, an emaciated teen may have lanugo hair – the teen needs to have frequent regular meals and needs to be inactive, so that her body can restore itself and her development can resume.

As a patient recovers, she will be allowed "passes" – these are small ways of trying out whether the patient is able to manage situations with less intense support than inside the hospital, since eventually she will be sent home. At first, passes will be for some time outside of the patient's room, then off the floor her room is on, then outside of the hospital building, then off hospital grounds, for an hour or a few hours. Eventually, if all goes well, she will be allowed overnight passes at home. During any pass that is long enough to include a snack or meal, the parents are advised to bring the patient back to hospital if she does not complete the food intake. This transitional phase back to the community is a good time for parents to begin taking over supervision of meals, by including one or more parent-supervised meals in hospital with a family therapist present to coach them through any difficulties.

Frequently or intermittently, the teen will check whether her family and staff *still* think she needs to be in hospital. Typically this will come up as a demand for longer passes, or to be discharged, rather than as a question, either the day before or at the weekly team meeting. Especially as the external indicators – energy level, weight, and mood – have improved, the teen may find it more difficult to attach significance to less visible ones – heart rate, blood pressure, and recovery of vital organs that may have lost mass due to starvation. If the heart rate still dips down into the forties at night, it is still too soon to be as active as in normal everyday life outside of the hospital.

CAN I LEAVE THE INPATIENT UNIT NOW?

Imagine you are a passenger on an airplane. You have to transfer planes at Heathrow in London. There they tell you that there is a delay due to engine trouble. Would you rather stay in the airport and wait the five hours it requires to repair the engine, or chance it, and get on the plane right away?

When it is time for the teen to leave the inpatient unit, the work of treating the eating disorder will continue on an outpatient basis, using family-based treatment, for six months to a year or more after discharge.

CASE EXAMPLE: GRAEME

Graeme is 14 years old and has lost 25 percent of his body weight rapidly over three months. He threatens suicide when asked to consider increasing his nutritional intake, counts calories, and is extremely concerned about fat. On examination, he presents with bradycardia (low heart rate), hypotension (low blood pressure), and prolonged QTc (heart arrhythmia). He refuses to eat anything whatsoever in hospital. Graeme appears guarded and depressed, and has isolated himself from other patients. Often he can be seen engaging in counting rituals and washing his hands.

Graeme is admitted to hospital because of the impact of rapid weight loss on his body systems, which are showing serious stress – he is medically unstable. In hospital, Graeme refuses to eat anything at all, and if he cannot be persuaded to change his mind he may need to be fed through a nasogastric tube, which will involve challenging his capacity to make decisions. In this case, his doctor may declare him incapable, which is to say that Graeme is unable to appreciate the impact of his health-related decisions on his life and is therefore not capable of making sound decisions in this area. In this case his parents will likely become substitute decision-makers and may then give consent for the tube feeding.

WHEN THE HEIMLICH MANEUVER DOESN'T WORK

When someone is choking and even the Heimlich maneuver (abdominal thrusts) does not work to clear the obstruction, the only way to give the person oxygen is to cut a small hole in the trachea.

When someone has not been eating for a long time, it is difficult for them to swallow and difficult for them to make a decision about whether to try swallowing. It is not a punishment to give them nutrition through a nasogastric tube. The person may die without food.

Many young people with eating disorders later say that having the tube feeding was a good thing at the time, because it relieved them of the unbearable responsibility for making a decision just then.

Because Graeme's feelings about eating anything more are so intense that he feels suicidal, he may benefit from a medication that makes him less anxious about eating and weight gain. The two types of medication that have been found helpful are SSRIs and atypical neuroleptics. Fluoxetine (Prozac) is an SSRI that is approved for use by the FDA in the United States and the MHRA in the United Kingdom with children and adolescents between the ages of 5 and 17; however, clinical evidence seems to suggest that it is not as effective with those who have very low weight. Atypical neuroleptics, including olanzapine and risperidone, are the ones that have been found helpful for children and teens respectively, when used in very small doses (Boachie, Goldfield and Spettigue 2003). However, there is evidence that they may cause prolongation of QTc interval, which is already prolonged in Graeme's case. If an atypical neuroleptic were to be tried with Graeme, he and his parents would need to be told about this risk. If they agreed to try the medication, adverse effects would be screened for, using a regular testing protocol. It is possible that Graeme also has OCD, given his counting rituals and handwashing. Medication could be helpful with this, as could be individual therapy, but the latter would more likely be helpful once he is out of the acute state he is in.

Graeme's parents will need to learn about the nature of eating disorders so that they can understand what their role will be in helping him to recover. He will be depending on them for this, and may need their support very directly at meals for up to a year or more. Once Graeme is medically stable and has reached his goal weight,[24] he may continue his recovery process in an outpatient setting, where his parents will continue to be involved and where any co-existing conditions, like OCD, will also be treated (Boachie and Jasper 2008).

Teens who have been inpatients more than once, or have failed to gain weight in an outpatient setting, should be considered for day hospital treatment. Their development is compromised by their lack of weight gain. It is important that they not be left in this limbo for

---

24 The goal weight will be a percentage of Graeme's "progress weight," i.e. the weight that Graeme would be now, had he not developed an eating disorder. The progress weight will be estimated by the pediatrician and dietitian, and will be based on Graeme's family history and his growth charts from early childhood on. Progress weight may be changed as a child gets older to reflect the natural developmental process of increasing weight with increasing height. The "goal" weight of an inpatient stay will be a percentage of the progress weight, and will be decided by the treatment team based on an estimate of what will give him the best chance of making a full recovery once he is outside of hospital.

long. Day hospital is attended by teens between the ages of 13 and 18, Monday through Friday for an average of six months.

All of the above would also apply to children with eating disorder not otherwise specified (EDNOS) and with bulimia. Usually when a child with bulimia is admitted, it is not about body weight but about electrolyte imbalance. The goal of the admission is to stabilize the patient medically while helping him or her to stop the binge–purge cycle, and then to restore electrolyte balance.

Chapter 8

The Recovery Process

There are normal ups and downs that are part of the recovery process and there are impediments to recovery. Parents' own willingness and ability to support their child can be limited by their understanding and appreciation of the potential dangers associated with the eating disorder, their wishes, and also their fears. For instance, a child who has been hospitalized and has benefitted enough from treatment to be discharged home to continue in outpatient treatment, may return to school and start getting very high marks again. Parents may fail to appreciate how serious the illness still is, even convince themselves that it is gone, and then stop providing the support the child needs to continue to get well. This leads to relapse. Alternatively, a child may make significant improvement through the efforts of all involved in her treatment and then assume greater responsibility for the maintenance of her own wellness. Parents' own understanding and appreciation of their child's stage in the recovery process may be out of sync with that of their child's. This situation may lead to the parents not trusting the child's genuine efforts to maintain improvement, leading again to relapse of the illness.

THE MOUNTAIN CLIMBER

When a child seems to be doing well, gaining weight, then suddenly loses some weight, the parents are disappointed.

This can be like a mountain climber who is almost at the summit, then has to drop down strategically before making a final push to the summit.

Understandably, parents would like the eating disorder to be gone. But sometimes a child has to appreciate how easy it is to lose weight and how difficult it is to gain it back in order to sustain the changes she makes.

Understanding the "stages of change"

As has been illustrated, the recovery process can be very complex and has many facets to it. This is one of the main reasons why a construct like "stages of change" helps facilitate our understanding and appreciation of the nature of recovery. The trans-theoretical model of change introduced by Prochaska, Norcross, and Diclemente (1995) identified six stages in the process of change: precontemplation, contemplation, preparation, action, maintenance, and termination. Because we are working with children and adolescents, we do not include the termination phase – parents will continue to be responsible until their children become adults.

CASE EXAMPLE: CHERYL

Cheryl is a teen with an eating disorder. She has been invited to a sleepover party with several friends of hers and is very excited about going. Cheryl tells her parents about the party and asks if she can attend. Her parents are aware that she has an eating disorder and are considering this as they talk to her about going. If Cheryl goes to the sleepover, she will be away from home for dinner, evening snack, breakfast, and possibly morning snack.

For each stage of change below, consider how you could handle the request in a way that will ensure Cheryl gets all of her needed nutrition.

Pre-contemplation

In pre-contemplation the person does not agree that she has a problem, even if her parents and doctor say that she does. This is popularly known as "denial." The person will likely get defensive if others bring up the problem, and will not talk about it with them. Because she doesn't see herself as having a problem, she won't consider initiating any changes in her behaviour.

Cheryl's parents need to consider that she will not be at home for dinner, evening snack, and breakfast. If they allow her to go to the sleepover, it is probable she will not eat enough food, or if she does, that she will compensate through exercise, or some form of purging. If she is bulimic, she might binge and purge at the party. If her parents bring up the issue of meals, Cheryl will likely say that it is not an issue and that she eats just like the other girls who will be there.

Would you give Cheryl permission to go to the sleepover? If yes, what safeguards, if any, would you implement?

Your answer:

To ensure that Cheryl gets the amount of nutrition that she needs, here are some possibilities you could consider.

- Refuse permission for Cheryl to attend the party altogether and monitor her meals and snacks, as well as potential compensating behaviours, at home.

- Allow Cheryl to go to the sleepover one hour after dinner, arrange for her to have evening snack earlier by distributing it over other meals or snacks of the day, and pick her up just before breakfast the next day.

- Allow Cheryl to attend some other portion of the party when she would not be missing any meals or snacks.

RED COAT, BLUE COAT

When your three-year-old child wants to go outside on a cold and snowy winter day, you might give her a choice about which winter jacket she wants to wear: the red one or the blue one – but you won't let her go outside without a winter jacket on.

When a child or teen with an eating disorder is in "pre-contemplation," she doesn't believe it matters whether she eats her meals or not. When she goes out with friends, she won't eat enough. You can give her limited choices, all of which ensure that she has what she needs, to protect her health and safety.

Contemplation

In the contemplation stage the person is aware that she has a problem and is struggling to understand it and how to deal with it. She would like to be free of the problem, but is not sure that she is ready or able to handle what would happen if she did (fears of failure, of giving up what is familiar, or of meeting new challenges). A person who is contemplating is thinking about change but has not yet committed to it.

Cheryl's parents again need to consider that if they allow her to go to the sleepover, she will not eat enough food; or if she does, that she will compensate through exercise or some form of purging. If she is bulimic, she might binge and purge at the party. If her parents bring up the issue of meals, Cheryl might be willing to discuss it with them, but it is likely that she will downplay the risk of missing meals or compensating. She might say, "It's just one night and all my friends will be there. It's Petra's birthday and I've never missed her birthday party. I will have something to eat [or, I won't purge]. Anyway, why are you making such a big deal about one dinner?"

Would you give Cheryl permission to go to the sleepover? If yes, what safeguards, if any, would you implement?

Your answer:

To ensure that Cheryl gets the amount of nutrition that she needs, here are some possibilities you could consider:

- Arrange for a trusted adult at the party to have a copy of Cheryl's meal plan, to monitor her meals and snacks, and watch for potential compensation. (This requires a willing and informed adult who knows that Cheryl has an eating disorder and who Cheryl knows is taking on this role.)

- Allow Cheryl to go to the sleepover one hour after dinner, arrange for her to have the evening snack earlier by distributing it over other meals or snacks of the day, and pick her up just before breakfast the next day.

- Allow Cheryl to choose a portion of the party she would most like to attend and arrange for her to have her meals and snacks before and after this period of time, so that she does not miss any nutrition.

See "The leaky raft" on p.80.

Preparation

Once a person has committed to making changes, she is in preparation. She can create plans and put specific steps toward change into practice. However, the fears she has about changing her behaviours may bring doubts that make her want to hide her plans from others or avoid making any dates to start them. She may feel that she can carry out a plan when she imagines it, but then find it overwhelmingly difficult to do so when it is time to put the plan into effect.

Cheryl's parents still need to consider that if they allow her to go to the sleepover, she will struggle to eat enough food or avoid compensating through exercise, or some other form of purging. If she is bulimic, she might binge and purge at the party. Since she is in preparation, Cheryl will be willing to discuss plans with them, but may not be able to carry out the plans on her own. She might say, "Yes, Mom and Dad, I will do it. I know I didn't do it last time, but things are different now. I know I have to eat and not compensate," but she may not be able to carry out this intention when she is with her friends. Something may happen that makes her feel excluded, leading her to feel negatively about her body, and then when she is served foods she finds scary, she may not be willing to eat them, or she may purge if she does.

Would you give Cheryl permission to go to the sleepover? If yes, what safeguards, if any, would you implement?

Your answer:

To ensure that Cheryl gets the amount of nutrition that she needs, make a plan together with her that includes back-up support. Here are some possibilities you could consider.

- Ask Cheryl to tell you her plans for how she will manage the meals and snacks she will have at the party. For example, she could call her friend Petra and ask what foods will be served at dinner, snack, and breakfast.
  - o Then discuss with Cheryl what difficulties or barriers could come up for her in relation to having these foods. For

example, if she is going to have birthday cake, will she feel pressure to have too little dinner?

o Then plan how you can act as a back-up so that she manages any difficulties that do come up. For example, text or call Cheryl after dinner and ask her to tell you what portions she had and if there have been any compensating behaviours – bring her home if needed so that she can complete the food she needs.

o If there is enough time before the sleepover, try having a similar meal sequence at home, to practice.

• Arrange for a trusted adult to check in with Cheryl periodically to watch for potential under-eating or compensation. (This requires a willing and informed adult who knows that Cheryl has an eating disorder, and who Cheryl knows is taking on this role.)

• Allow Cheryl to attend the party, except for any portion that is likely to be too challenging for her and where there is no workable back-up plan. For example, if she finds breakfast and snacks easy to manage, she might have dinner at home and go to the party after the dinner and birthday cake have been served, and stay for the rest of the sleepover.

SOLO SUBWAY RIDE

When your child turned 12 and her new school was several subway stops away from home, she needed help learning how to use the subway to get there. First you went all the way from home to the school along with her, showing her what to do. Next time you went along with her and let her show you what to do. Then you went ahead of her and met her outside the subway station near her school. Finally you went to work and she called you using her cell phone when she arrived at school. If any of these steps did not work out the way they should, you repeated them until they did.

A teen with an eating disorder who is preparing to eat of her own accord may need to practice over and over with clear plans and back-up support to get her to her destination.

Action

A person who is in the action phase is regularly putting the plans she made in the preparation phase into motion. She accepts help willingly and asks for it when she is feeling hesitant or at risk – for example, when facing a difficult or challenging situation. The person in action looks for friends who will support her new behaviours and rewards herself when she accomplishes a plan.

Cheryl's parents can be sure that if they allow her to go to the sleepover, she will be honest with them about whether she expects the party to be challenging and needs some support to eat enough food, to avoid compensating through exercise or some other form of purging, or to avoid bingeing and purging.

Would you give Cheryl permission to go to the sleepover? If yes, what safeguards, if any, would you implement?

Your answer:

To support Cheryl in a way that recognizes the progress she has made and the responsibility she is taking, without taking the view that at this stage she should be able to manage by herself, you could consider checking in with Cheryl about the sleepover and asking her if she anticipates any difficulties. If she does:

- offer your support in planning it out, or

- be available if she wants you to be her support person.

THE FRENCH TUTOR

When a teen is in Grade 12 and not doing well in French, you don't say "Come on, you're in Grade 12, get on with it. I'm not getting you a tutor!" You find a tutor to help her with French. You don't get her a tutor for every subject, just the subject she is struggling with.

Similarly, when a teen is recovering from an eating disorder and she is managing most situations without supervision but struggling with restaurant meals, you don't have to assume that she should be able to handle it, nor do you have to revert to total supervision. Just find a way to support her when there is going to be a restaurant meal.

Maintenance

The person who is in maintenance has been putting her commitment to change into practice for months. She continues to practice new behaviours and routinely evaluates what is working well and what no longer helps her. She is committed to sustaining new behaviours.

Cheryl's parents can be confident that if they allow her to go to the sleepover, she will eat enough food and will not compensate, nor will she binge and purge.

What safeguards, if any, would you implement?

Your answer:

At this stage, Cheryl's parents may need to be more concerned with curfews and substance use, balancing homework and a part-time job, or other issues like driving the family car. While they no longer need to be "on Cheryl's back," they must still "watch her back," especially at times of significant stress, so that relapses can be identified early on and prevented.

In the process of change, people do not usually move through the stages in a straight linear fashion. They go back and forth between the stages along the way to recovery and it is common for there to be relapses.

"Stages of change," as illustrated above, usually describes the motivational changes as observed in the identified patient. However, in our daily practice we are frequently faced either with situations where the teen has moved on very well and is ready to take next steps forward, or with situations where the teen is not ready to take the next steps forward. In the former case, a teen may be stuck because her parents are lagging behind in their understanding of the nature of the recovery process; or in the latter case, they may simply not believe that their child's illness is serious enough to warrant the kind of commitment therapists are requiring of them. This may lead to the child seriously relapsing. This phenomenon can result in major inhibition in the progress of young people with eating disorders, such that we feel it warrants serious attention. Since in these cases the young person's lack of progress results mainly from the parents' limited understanding or appreciation of what recovery is like, we feel it is necessary to bring attention to the *stages of change of the parents.* We propose that we refer to this phenomenon as "stages of change by proxy."

Questions and answers

Q: *Our teen seems to vacillate between pre-contemplation and contemplation. We always have to give her "limited choices" about what she eats and we do not negotiate amounts, rather we put the serving on her plate. There is always one of us with her at meals and snacks. She used to be the sweetest girl in the world, always doing what we wanted her to do. Now it is as if she has been taken over by a malevolent force: she yells at us, calls us names, sometimes throws things, and threatens to run away. What should we do?*

152

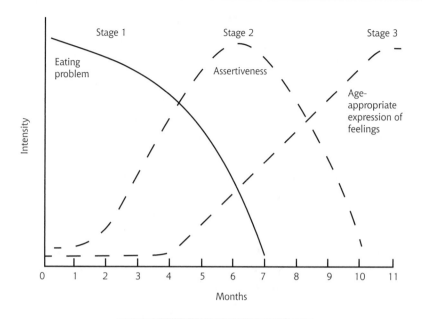

Figure 8.1: Stages of illness and recovery
*Reprinted from Lask and Bryant-Waugh 1993, p.134, with
permission of the authors and Taylor and Francis*

In whatever type of treatment a young person is involved, she will go through a period of intense behavioural protest against the treatment, once it begins to succeed at helping her to eat (Lask and Bryant-Waugh 2007). She will not like gaining weight – even if at some level she knows she must, and is secretly relieved that her parents are helping her to do so. During this period of time, which may be most intense for about three months, but can continue for up to six months or more, it is likely that she will be angry and possibly aggressive with her parents, deceptive about her eating practices, and will try to "scam" when having her weight taken. For instance, she may drink copious amounts before being weighed, or fix small but heavy items onto her body so that she appears to weigh more than she does. It is important that the family doctor or pediatrician has experience with eating disorders and takes precautions against these deceptions. It is also helpful if the teen is not informed of her weight.

The intensity of "assertiveness" increases as the eating disorder symptoms are challenged. Dr. Bryan Lask and Dr. Rachel Bryant-Waugh have written about this part of the recovery from an eating disorder:

> If your child is to make a full recovery she will most likely go through a phase that you will probably find extremely difficult. This is a very trying phase indeed. She will be horrible to you and probably to us as well. You will be angry with us, and feel that we have made her worse. However, we will be pleased because this will mean that she is getting better. It is as if she has been unable to express these feelings and they have built up inside her almost to the point when she cannot eat. Once treatment starts, however, these feelings will come pouring out, almost like a volcano exploding. We will of course do our best to support you during this stage and it will come to an end. However, if you block her feelings, if you don't let her express them, or you punish her, she will withdraw and lock them up inside. You may then feel better but her eating problems won't resolve. Of course, you will need to set limits such as no breaking things or physical violence, but if you can tolerate the rest you will be helping her to recover. (Lask and Bryant-Waugh 2007, p.173)

Q: *We are giving our son the right amount of food, but he is not gaining weight. Why?*

It may be that your child just needs more food, but it could be that he is not eating all of the food that you are giving him, or he is finding ways to compensate for the food later on – for example, by exercising or by purging. At meals, the child or teen may try to eat less than he needs by keeping his parents at a distance so that they cannot see what he eats, by hiding food, or crumbling it. If his parents close this gap, then he may simply refuse the food or vehemently argue with parents about the food until they tire and relent. All of these behaviours are expressions of the young person's fear of giving up his illness and are to be expected, but not accepted. At meals it is helpful to keep conversation light and to watch for hiding of food. Meals and snacks should take place within a specific time frame and a plan should be made with professional help regarding how to deal with food refusals.

Parents also need to monitor washroom use and shower use for about an hour after meals or snacks.

Q: *"She has stopped purging"... "She's not fainting anymore"... "She's talking to us again." Doesn't that mean she is recovered now?*

No, whilst stopping purging is a great achievement, this does not mean that she is free of the eating disorder. The purging may be quickly replaced by restriction, laxative abuse, or excessive exercise. Not fainting may mean that there is improvement, but does not mean that she is fully weight-restored, and there may be organs that are still at risk. That she is talking to you again means that you are on the right track and should continue working together.

Q: *It seems like nothing is happening – we have been doing everything you tell us to do, but nothing is changing, she still won't do it on her own.*

THE AIRPLANE TRIP ACROSS THE OCEAN

Look at a Boeing 747 airplane. A little tiny truck driven by a man pulls it out of the hangar. After the passengers get on, it moves out from the dock very slowly – you could still run beside it. Then it goes faster and faster and you can hear it roar as it takes off. It's going too fast now to keep up with it. It pushes hard, defying gravity. As it reaches cruising height and speed, things change again. Pretty soon it feels like nothing is happening, at an altitude of 38,000 feet. This is the longest part of your journey across the Atlantic. Cruising at the same height and speed with nothing apparently happening. All of a sudden, there is turbulence. Suddenly you remember how fast you are going and how far you are from the ground. The turbulence passes and you cruise again for several hours. Then the pilot announces that you will be landing at Heathrow and are beginning the descent. Again you recognize the speed at which you are travelling. Then you land! You realize how far you have come.

With an eating disorder there can be a very long phase where it seems that you are just repeating and repeating what you are doing, with nothing happening. Still you need to keep on doing it, over and over again. It is not always easy to appreciate on an ongoing basis the progress you are making in the recovery process. It does not mean you are not making any. You sometimes only appreciate the progress at the end of the journey.

Q: *My daughter has been eating well for several months now, with no bingeing or purging, but she still dislikes her body and makes disparaging comments about being fat. What is wrong?*

Body dissatisfaction is often a precursor of an eating disorder – that is to say that it is present even before normal eating behaviours change. It is also probably the last thing to improve, even after the eating disorder symptoms are resolved. This may be because it is usually after the symptoms are resolved that the issues that underlay the eating disorder surface again.

FEELING FAT AND A VISIT TO THE DENTIST

It's a little like being at the dentist. You get a needle for anesthesia and it freezes a part of your mouth. It feels like your whole face has become huge. (If you look in the mirror you can see that it has not.) Someone teases you and you feel more self-conscious.

You have tooth decay and it hurts. When you don't want to deal with the pain, you keep it numb. But if you deal with it, you can chew again.

If your daughter believes she is fat and still eats enough, you know that she is okay, that is, she can function normally. However, you will still need to watch her back.

THE ASTHMA ATTACK AND THE INHALER

A child with an acute asthma attack will need to be taken to hospital. Once she is better, she will still need to keep an inhaler in case another attack is induced.

Similarly, with an eating disorder: once your child is doing well, if you watch her back, it will help her to continue doing well.

Q: *Our daughter was in a highly structured eating disorder program for six months. After two weeks outside the program, she started losing weight again. She told us not to worry because it is normal to lose a bit of weight after leaving* *a program, and that the program goal weight includes a "buffer" so that it won't matter if you lose some weight. Should we be worried?*

One of the indicators of poor outcome is when someone starts losing weight shortly after successfully leaving a highly structured program. If they drop any weight in the first four weeks or so, and this is not reversed immediately, the pattern of weight loss is likely to continue and compared with those who do not lose weight in this initial period, there is a strong chance that within two years' time the person will have relapsed completely (Woodside 2007).

Q: *My son is accepting the weight gain, but he struggles because the weight he has gained is all fat and not muscle. I've encouraged him to start lifting weights again. How about exercise? Isn't it healthy to start exercising once you get to your goal weight?*

Exercise on its own is healthy for everybody, but in this case the feeling your son has that all the weight he has gained is fat, is because the initial weight gain goes to his vital organs. Excessive exercise is one of the most difficult symptoms to get rid of. Exercise should be re-introduced in a very controlled fashion, in consultation with your treatment team.

Q: *We didn't agree with the doctors in the program our daughter was in. They wanted her to gain to a weight she had never been to before. So we took her out of the program and will continue to help her at home. We had to sign some papers saying that we were taking her out of the program "against medical advice." What does it mean?*

When you sign your child out of hospital against medical advice, you are indicating that you have been told by your doctor and understand that his or her advice is to keep your child in the hospital because there is a serious medical risk attached to removing the child too soon. You are taking responsibility for this decision and may be forfeiting your child's place in a program (and will have to re-apply if you change your mind).

It is important to consider that a child who has had an eating disorder may need to gain to a weight she has never reached previously, because she should also have grown in height during the time she was ill and will need to have a weight that supports this height. (See the

"Sending a rocket to the moon" analogy on p.47.) Another way to think about it is this: if your child became ill at age 11 and recovered at age 16, would you be satisfied if her brain was stuck at the level of development it had reached when she was 11?

Q: *Our daughter was doing very well in the day hospital program she was in. We wanted to take her out of the program at the end of August so that she could start school with her friends in September. The staff of the program would not give her a "graduation" because they wanted her to maintain her progress weight for a few more weeks. Why are they so picky?*

An eating disorder can be a career-ending disorder. It can end in death and it can become chronically debilitating. Without recovery, there will be no school success and there will be few, if any, relationships with friends that survive. The staff were saying that there is nothing more important at this stage of recovery than your daughter's life, and there are no short cuts to recovery. Starting back to school with a small foothold on recovery, your daughter will be vulnerable to relapse. Be sure to keep supporting her fully as she makes this transition.

Q: *I'm still depressed (or anxious). How is your medication even going to help me with my depression or anxiety?*

It is believed that when you are depressed or anxious your serotonin levels go down or get used up too quickly, so that you are not able to process information effectively. The medication ensures that the serotonin is in the right place at the right time.

CONTACT LENSES AND GLASSES

A person has to wear glasses. She prefers to wear contact lenses. At night she takes out her disposable lenses and throws them away. In the morning she puts new ones in. What will she do if she has to take them out because they are irritating, or she runs out of contact lenses and has to order new ones? She will continue to use her old glasses until she can wear the contacts again.

Similarly, the medication prevents serotonin from being removed from your system. As your body recovers from the eating disorder, your brain will find a way to maintain the levels of serotonin needed and you may be able to discontinue using the medication.

Q: *Our daughter is now at normal weight and is not compensating. Why should we still be watching her?*

Parents can still be very helpful in helping their children maintain wellness.

A LASTING RESPONSIBILITY

When you buy a house, it becomes yours. However, in Canada, the person who sold it to you is responsible for some time afterward for fixing certain problems if they occur.

Chapter 9

Conclusion

Early identification and treatment of eating disorders in children and adolescents is vital for minimizing the potential impacts of the illness on their physical, psychological, social, and emotional development. Parents are the best resource in children's recovery. The earlier parents put full focus on managing their child with an eating disorder, the better their chances for success. Those with eating disorders may take many years to seek treatment on their own and may find it very difficult to complete treatment after they start it, but parents of children and adolescents with eating disorders can bring them to treatment sooner, encourage and support them through the treatment, and continue to provide support after formal treatment has been completed. Guilt and self-blame have no place because parents do not cause eating disorders – and they are simply invaluable in recovery. Although a significant number of those who develop eating disorders may become chronically ill and there is a potentially high mortality rate, professionals working closely with parents and their children can help reduce these outcomes by supporting parents to persist until their children are able to take over.

With eating disorders, patience and persistence may be the reason why children get well. Trying to speed through or take short cuts with the recovery process to minimize costs or quickly get a child back to school, may actually slow down or stop the recovery. This is illustrated by the symbolic gift (see Figure 9.1 on the following page) that one young person gave to staff when she left the program. It was an elephant with a little elephant inside, carved from soapstone. She said the eating disorder starts slowly and takes you over, making you feel as if you are a big elephant. Your parents and others tell you that you are not big, that you are very delicate and small, like the little elephant. But you are stuck inside, feeling huge, with darkness all around you. It seems as if everyone who says they are trying to help you is really trying to hurt you. Everything you have to eat, everything they say will help you, seems like it is turning you into a big elephant. Gradually, as she recovered, this young person saw herself as she really was: an independent person who could communicate for herself and reach out for support from all those who were always there supporting her.

Figure 9.1: With persistence and a gentle touch

With patience and the ability to tolerate the ups and downs of the illness, parents can help their children recover.

The analogies and metaphors in this book are by no means exhaustive. This is an attempt to introduce a new way of increasing understanding and appreciation of eating disorders that will allay parents' guilt and anxiety and enhance their ability to work together with healthcare providers to defeat the illness. So please create your own analogies and metaphors!

Appendix I

Current Diagnostic Criteria

Anorexia nervosa, bulimia nervosa and EDNOS

Below are the current diagnostic criteria for anorexia nervosa, bulimia nervosa, and eating disorder not otherwise specified (EDNOS), as stated in the DSM-IV-TR and the ICD-10.

All material from DSM-IV-TR is reprinted from the *Diagnostic and Statistical Manual of Mental Disorders* (4th ed.), Text Revision (© 2000), with permission from the American Psychiatric Association.

a) DSM-IV-TR: Anorexia Nervosa

A. Refusal to maintain body weight at or above a minimally normal weight for age and height (e.g. weight loss leading to maintenance of body weight less than 85 percent of that expected; or failure to make expected weight gain during period of growth, leading to body weight less than 85 percent of that expected).

B. Intense fear of gaining weight or becoming fat, even though underweight.

C. Disturbance in the way in which one's body weight or shape is experienced, undue influence of body weight or shape on self-evaluation, or denial of the seriousness of the current low body weight.

D. In postmenarcheal females, amenorrhea, i.e., the absence of at least three consecutive menstrual cycles. (A woman is considered to have amenorrhea if her periods occur only following hormone, e.g. estrogen, administration.)

Select type:

Restricting type: during the current episode of anorexia nervosa, the person has not regularly engaged in binge-eating or purging behavior (i.e. self-induced vomiting or the misuse of laxatives, diuretics, or enemas).

Binge-eating/purging type: during the current episode of anorexia nervosa, the person has regularly engaged in binge-eating or purging behavior (i.e. self-induced vomiting or the misuse of laxatives, diuretics, or enemas).

(American Psychiatric Association 2000)

b) DSM-IV-TR: Bulimia Nervosa

A. Recurrent episodes of binge-eating characterized by both:

- eating, in a discrete period of time (e.g. within any two-hour period), an amount of food that is definitely larger than most people would eat during a similar period of time and under similar circumstances

- a sense of lack of control over eating during the episode, defined by a feeling that one cannot stop eating or control what or how much one is eating.

B. Recurrent inappropriate compensatory behavior to prevent weight gain:

- Self-induced vomiting.

- Misuse of laxatives, diuretics, enemas, or other medications.

- Fasting.

- Excessive exercise.

C. The binge-eating and inappropriate compensatory behavior both occur, on average, at least twice a week for three months.

D. Self-evaluation is unduly influenced by body shape and weight.

E. The disturbance does not occur exclusively during episodes of anorexia nervosa.

Select type:

Purging type: during the current episode of bulimia nervosa, the person has regularly engaged in self-induced vomiting or the misuse of laxatives, diuretics, or enemas.

Non-purging type: during the current episode of bulimia nervosa, the person has used inappropriate compensatory behavior but has not regularly engaged in self-induced vomiting or misused laxatives, diuretics, or enemas.

(American Psychiatric Association 2000)

c) DSM-IV-TR: EDNOS (Eating Disorder Not Otherwise Specified)

Eating disorder not otherwise specified includes disorders of eating that do not meet the criteria for any specific eating disorder.

1. For female patients, all of the criteria for anorexia nervosa are met except that the patient has regular menses.

2. All of the criteria for anorexia nervosa are met except that, despite significant weight loss, the patient's current weight is in the normal range.

3. All of the criteria for bulimia nervosa are met except that the binge-eating and inappropriate compensatory mechanisms occur less than twice a week or for less than three months.

4. The patient has normal body weight and regularly uses inappropriate compensatory behavior after eating small amounts of food (e.g. self-induced vomiting after consuming two cookies).

5. Repeatedly chewing and spitting out, but not swallowing, large amounts of food.

Binge-eating disorder is recurrent episodes of binge-eating in the absence of regular inappropriate compensatory behavior characteristic of bulimia nervosa.

(American Psychiatric Association 2000)

All material from ICD-10 is reprinted from ICD-10 Version 2007, *Classification of Mental and Behavioural Disorders: Diagnostic Criteria for Research* (© 2007), with permission from the World Health Organization.

F50.0 Anorexia Nervosa

A disorder characterized by deliberate weight loss, induced and sustained by the patient. It occurs most commonly in adolescent girls and young women, but adolescent boys and young men may also be affected, as may children approaching puberty and older women up to the menopause. The disorder is associated with a specific psychopathology whereby a dread of fatness and flabbiness of body contour persists as an intrusive overvalued idea, and the patients impose a low weight threshold on themselves. There is usually undernutrition of varying severity with secondary endocrine and metabolic changes and disturbances of bodily function. The symptoms include restricted dietary choice, excessive exercise, induced vomiting and purgation, and use of appetite suppressants and diuretics.

Excludes: loss of appetite (R63.0); psychogenic (F50.8)

(World Health Organization 2007)

F50.1 Atypical Anorexia Nervosa

Disorders that fulfill some of the features of anorexia nervosa but in which the overall clinical picture does not justify that diagnosis. For instance, one of the key symptoms, such as amenorrhoea or marked dread of being fat, may be absent in the presence of marked weight loss and weight-reducing behaviour. This diagnosis should not be made in the presence of known physical disorders associated with weight loss.

(World Health Organization 2007)

F50.2 Bulimia Nervosa

A syndrome characterized by repeated bouts of overeating and an excessive preoccupation with the control of body weight, leading to a pattern of overeating followed by vomiting or use of purgatives. This disorder shares many psychological features with anorexia nervosa, including an overconcern with body shape and weight. Repeated vomiting is likely to give rise to disturbances of body electrolytes and physical complications. There is often, but not always, a history of an earlier episode of anorexia nervosa, the interval ranging from a few months to several years.

(World Health Organization 2007)

F50.3 Atypical Bulimia Nervosa

Disorders that fulfill some of the features of bulimia nervosa, but in which the overall clinical picture does not justify that diagnosis. For instance, there may be recurrent bouts of overeating and overuse of purgatives without significant weight change, or the typical overconcern about body shape and weight may be absent.

(World Health Organization 2007)

Other conditions

There are also other conditions that require management similar to that for an eating disorder. The following are non-official proposed criteria for other eating issues among children.

a) Food Avoidance Emotional Disorder (FAED)

This is a disorder of the emotions in which food avoidance is a prominent symptom in the presenting complaint.

- A history of food avoidance or difficulty (e.g. food fads or restrictions).

- A failure to meet the criteria for anorexia nervosa.
- The absence of organic brain disease, psychosis, illicit drug abuse, or prescribed drug-related side-effects.
- Mood disturbance in the form of mild depression, anxiety, obsessionality, or phobias especially for specific foods.
- Weight loss.
- Determined food avoidance.
- No distorted view of their own weight or shape.
- Not preoccupied with weight or shape.

(Bryant-Waugh 2000, pp.33–4; Higgs, Goodyer and Birch 1989)

b) Selective eating

- Food intake limited to a very narrow range of preferred foods.
- Attempts to widen the repertoire are usually met with extreme resistance and distress.
- Usually child is of normal height and weight for age (growth not adversely affected).
- More boys than girls.
- No preoccupation with weight or shape.
- No distortion of own body size.
- No prominent fear of choking or gagging.
- No need to intervene unless it has an adverse effect on social, physical, or emotional development.

(Bryant-Waugh 2000, p.34)

c) Restrictive eating

- Never seem to eat very large amounts nor express much interest or enjoyment in food.

- No evidence of mood disturbance.

- Tend to be small and light but within normal range of variation.

- Eat normal range and types of food, but do not eat very much.

- No body image distortion.

- No preoccupation with weight or shape.

- May need supplementation around puberty to support continued growth.

(Bryant-Waugh 2000, p.35)

d) Food refusal

- Common phenomenon in younger children.

- In older children, food refusers tend to reserve refusal for one or two particular people or situations.

- Usually represents a difficulty in the direct expression of existing concerns or uncertainties.

- No body image distortion.

- No preoccupation with weight or shape.

- Tend not to have weight problems.

- May interfere with the quality of relationships with the child.

(Bryant-Waugh 2000, p.36)

e) Functional dysphagia

- Food avoidance.

- Fear of swallowing, choking, or vomiting.

- Usually there is a clear precipitant in the form of an adverse event, e.g. food poisoning.

- No abnormal cognition regarding weight and/or shape.

- No morbid pre-occupation with weight and/or shape.

(Bryant-Waugh 2000, p.36)

f) Pervasive refusal syndrome

1. Profound refusal to eat, drink, walk, talk, or self-care.

2. Underweight and often dehydrated.

3. Determined resistance to efforts to help.

4. Tends not to be communicating sufficiently to ascertain whether cognitive criteria for anorexia nervosa are fulfilled.

5. Refusal extends to all areas of social and emotional functioning (not the case in anorexia nervosa).

6. May be life-threatening.

(Lask et al. 1991; Bryant-Waugh 2000, pp.36–7)

g) Appetite loss secondary to depression

Loss of appetite is well known to be a symptom of depression.

1. Social withdrawal may occur.

2. No preoccupation with weight and shape.

3. No body image distortion.

4. No determined avoidance of food.

With children, the relationship between eating and mood disorder may be more complex than in adults.

(Bryant-Waugh 2000, pp.37–8)

h) Pediatric Autoimmune Neuropsychiatric Disorders Associated with Streptococcal infection (PANDAS)

Includes a very rare form of eating disorder that is currently being considered as a possible official diagnostic category.

PANDAS: Hypothesized criteria for PANDAS – anorexia nervosa

Prepubertal onset of anorexia nervosa

1. Acute onset and/or symptom exacerbation of anorexia nervosa.

2. Evidence of antecedent or concomitant streptococcal infection.

   o positive throat culture

   o positive serological findings (elevated antibody titre).

3. Increased psychiatric symptoms that do not occur exclusively during stress or physical illness.

4. Concomitant neurological abnormalities, with motor hyperactivity and/or adventitious movements: "If you do not see piano-playing choreiform movements in the fingers, then it's probably not PANDAS" (Puxley et al. 2008, p.19).

At present no biological markers reliably distinguish PANDAS from typical childhood onset anorexia nervosa (Puxley et al. 2008). There is "established evidence for streptococcal infections being responsible for a number of other conditions including ARF, Sydenhams's Chorea, tics/Tourette's syndrome, and OCD" (Puxley et al. 2008, p.17).

If PANDAS is suspected, the clinician should obtain a throat culture and streptococcal antibody titre – if negative, carefully monitor the patient for subsequent infections (Puxley et al. 2008, p.20).

Appendix II

List of Analogies and Metaphors

Glossary

AV junction Atrioventricular junction, an electrical transmission complex in the middle of the heart. When the heart rate drops below 60 beats per minute, but is above 40, it is usually this complex that takes over control of the heartbeat.

Bradycardia Slow heart rate, that is, a rate lower than 60 beats per minute.

Ferritin A ubiquitous intracellular protein that stores iron and releases it in a controlled fashion. If ferritin levels are low, this will affect the level of iron in the blood.

FSH Follicle-stimulating hormone, regulates the development, growth, pubertal maturation, and reproductive processes of the body. FSH and LH act synergistically in reproduction.

Hermatemesis Vomiting of blood.

Lanugo hair Fine downy hair normally seen on fetuses or newborns. It may also be seen on the arms and chests of females with anorexia.

LH Lutenizing hormone, produced by the pituitary gland. In *females*, an acute rise of LH, called the LH surge, triggers ovulation.

Non-focal abdominal pain Pain that is not restricted to one specific area of the abdomen.

Perioral irritation Irritation of the skin around the mouth.

Petechiae Fine red or purple spots on the body caused by a minor hemorrhage.

QTc interval Technical term that indicates a problem in the heart, especially in the context of bradycardia (low heart rate). In the context of eating disorders, people with this condition are more likely to have a heart attack if it is not corrected.

SA node Sinus atrial node, the impulse-generating (pacemaker) tissue located in the right atrium of the heart, and thus the generator of normal heart rhythm (60–100 beats per minute).

sTSH A blood test that helps endocrinologists determine whether their patients are experiencing thyroid problems.

References

Academy for Eating Disorders (2009) *Prevalence of Eating Disorders*. Deerfield, IL: Academy for Eating Disorders. Accessed on 24 April 2009 at www.aedweb. org

Agrawal, S. and Lask, B. (2009) "Neuroscience of anorexia nervosa: state of the art." *Pediatric Health 3*, 3, 209–212.

American Psychiatric Association (2000) *Diagnostic and Statistical Manual of Mental Disorders: DSM-IV-TR*. Washington, DC: American Psychiatric Association.

American Psychiatric Association (2006) *Practice Guidelines for the Treatment of Patients with Eating Disorders* (3rd ed.). Washington, DC: American Psychiatric Association.

Andersen, A.E. (1999) "Medical information for non-medical clinicians and educators treating patients with eating disorders: Psychotherapists, educators, nutritionists, experiential therapists, coaches." In P. Mehler and A. Andersen (eds) *Eating Disorders: A Guide to Medical Care and Complications*. Baltimore, MD: Johns Hopkins University Press.

Asen, E. and Scholz, M. (2010) *Multi-Family Therapy*. London and New York: Routledge Taylor & Francis Group.

Bainbridge, C. (2009) *Gifted Children and Asynchronous Development*. New York: About.com. Accessed on 18 April 2009 at http://giftedkids.about.com.

Baran, S.A., Weltzin, T.E. and Kaye, W.H. (1995) "Low discharge weight and outcome in anorexia nervosa." *The American Journal of Psychiatry 152*, 1070–1072.

Becker, A., Burwell, R.A., Gilman, S.E., Herzog, D.B. and Hamburg, P. (2002) "Eating behaviors and attitudes following prolonged exposure to television among ethnic Fijian adolescent girls." *British Journal of Psychiatry 180*, 509–514.

Bell, R. (1985) *Holy Anorexia*. Chicago, IL: University of Chicago Press.

Bennett, D., Sharpe, M., Freeman, C. and Carson, A. (2004) "Anorexia nervosa among female secondary school students in Ghana." *British Journal of Psychiatry 185*, 312–317.

Blinder, B.J., Cumella, E.J. and Sanathara, V.A. (2006) "Psychiatric comorbidities of female inpatients with eating disorders." *Psychosomatic Medicine 68*, 454–462.

Boachie, A. and Jasper, K. (2005) "What are the myths and misconceptions about eating disorders?" In D. Katzman and L. Pinhas (eds) *Help for Eating Disorders: A Parent's Guide to Symptoms, Causes and Treatments.* Toronto: Robert Rose Inc.

Boachie, A. and Jasper, K. (2006) "Helping adolescents with the social and psychological consequences of obesity." *The Ontario Medical Review: Journal of the Ontario Medical Association 73*, 11, 23–27.

Boachie, A. and Jasper, K. (2008) "When dieting courts disorder." *The Child and Family Journal 11*, 3, 14–22.

Boachie, A., Girz, L. and LaFrance, A. (2010) "Adolescent and parent outcomes following family-based day treatment for an eating disorder." Paper presented at the International Conference on Eating Disorders, Salzberg, Austria, June 7.

Boachie, A., Goldfield, G.S. and Spettigue, W. (2003) "Olanzapine use as an adjunctive treatment for hospitalized children with anorexia nervosa: Case reports." *International Journal of Eating Disorders 33*, 1, 98–103.

Bordo, S. (2004) *Unbearable Weight.* Berkeley and Los Angeles, CA: University of California Press.

Brown, C. and Jasper, K. (1993) "Why women? Why weight? Why now?" In C. Brown and K. Jasper (eds) *Consuming Passions: Feminist Approaches to Weight Preoccupation and Eating Disorders.* Toronto: Second Story Press.

Brumberg, J.J. (1988) *Fasting Girls: The Emergence of Anorexia Nervosa as a Modern Disease.* Cambridge, MA: Harvard University Press.

Bryant-Waugh, R. (2000) "Eating disorders in children: An overview." In B. Lask and R. Bryant-Waugh (eds) *Anorexia Nervosa and Related Eating Disorders in Children and Adolescents.* Hove: Psychology Press.

Bryant-Waugh, R., Lask, B., Shafran, R.L. and Fosson, A.R. (1992) "Do doctors recognize eating disorders in children?" *Archives of Disease in Childhood 67*, 103–105.

Bulik, C.M. (2004) "Genetic and biological risk factors." In J.K. Thompson (ed.) *The Handbook of Eating Disorders and Obesity.* Hoboken, NJ: Wiley.

Carter, J.C., Blackmore, E., Sutandar-Pinnock, K. and Woodside, B. (2004) "Relapse in anorexia nervosa: A survival analysis." *Psychological Medicine 34*, 671–679.

Chui, H.T., Christensen, B., Zipursky, R., Richards, B.A., *et al.* (2008) "Cognitive function and brain structure in females with a history of adolescent-onset anorexia nervosa." *Pediatrics 122,* e426–e437.

Cochrane, C.E. (1998) "Eating regulation, responses, and eating disorders." In G.W. Stuart and S.I. Sundeen (eds) *Principles and Practice of Psychiatric Nursing* (6th ed.). St Louis, MI: Mosby.

Connan, F., Lightman, S.L., Landau, S., Wheeler, M., Treasure, J. and Campbell, I.C. (2007) "An investigation of hypothalamic-pituitary-adrenal axis hyperactivity in anorexia nervosa: The role of CRH and AVP." *Journal of Psychiatric Research 41,* 1–2, 131–143.

DeSocio, J.E., O'Toole, J.K., Nemirow, S.J., Lukach, M.E. and Magee, M.G. (2006) "Screening for childhood eating disorders in primary care." *Primary Care Companion to the Journal of Clinical Psychiatry 9,* 1, 16–20.

Dubin, D. (2000) *Rapid Interpretation of EKGs* (6th ed.). Tampa, FL: Cover Publishing Co.

Eisenberg, M.E., Neumark-Sztainer, D. and Story, M. (2003) "Associations of weight-based teasing and emotional well-being among adolescents." *Archives of Pediatric and Adolescent Medicine 157,* 8, 733–738.

Eisler, I. (2005) "The empirical and theoretical base of family therapy and multiple family day therapy for adolescent anorexia nervosa." *Journal of Family Therapy 27,* 104–131.

Favaro, A. and Santonastaso, P. A. (1997) "Suicidality in eating disorders: Clinical and psychological correlates." *Acta Psychiatrica Scandinavica 95,* 6, 508–514.

Francis, L.A. and Birch, L.L. (2005) "Maternal weight status modulates the effects of restriction on daughters' eating and weight." *International Journal of Obesity 29,* 942–949.

Geary, J. (2009) *Metaphorically Speaking.* New York: TED.com. Accessed on 15 January 2011 at www.ted.com.

Grewal, S., Jasper, K., Steinegger, C., Yu, E. and Boachie, A. (2011) "Factors associated with completion of a day hospital program for adolescents with eating disorders." Paper presented at the International Conference on Eating Disorders, Miami, Florida, April 30.

Harden, J. (2005) "Parenting a young person with mental health problems: Temporal disruption and reconstruction." *Sociology of Health and Illness 3,* 351–371.

Herrin, M. and Matsumoto, N. (2007) *The Parent's Guide to Eating Disorders.* Carslbad, CA: Gürze Books.

Higgs, J., Goodyer, I. and Birch, J. (1989) "Anorexia nervosa and food avoidance emotional disorder." *Archives of Disease in Childhood 64,* 346–351.

Jasper, K. (2007) "The blinding power of genetics: Manufacturing and privatizing stories of eating disorders." In C. Brown and T. Augusta-Scott (eds) *Narrative Therapy: Making Meaning, Making Lives.* Thousand Oaks, CA: Sage Publications Inc.

Jasper, K. and Boachie, A. (2007) "Living with an eating disorder: What about brothers and sisters?" *NEDIC Bulletin 22,* 4 (National Eating Disorders Information Centre, Canada).

Jasper, K., Boachie, A. and Lafrance, A. (2009) "Family-based therapy for children and adolescents with eating disorders." *NEDIC Bulletin 24,* 5.

Jasper, K., Boachie, A. and Lafrance, A. (2010) "Multi-family group therapy for children and adolescents with eating disorders." *NEDIC Bulletin 25,* 3.

Katzman, D.K., Lambe, E.K., Mikulis, D.J., Ridgley, J.N., Goldbloom, D.S. and Zipursky, R. (1996) "Cerebral gray matter and white matter volume deficits in adolescent girls with anorexia nervosa." *The Journal of Pediatrics 129,* 6, 794–803.

Kaye, W.H., Nagata, T., Weltzin, T.E., Hsu, B., *et al.* (2001) "Double-blind placebo-controlled administration of fluoxetine in restricting- and restricting-purging-type anorexia nervosa.' *Biological Psychiatry 49,* 644–652.

Klump, K. (2009, February 7) *Nature vs. Nurture, Genes or Environment: Why Do Eating Disorders Develop?* Toronto: Sheena's Place Forum for Eating Disorders Awareness Week.

Klump, K., Bulik, C., Kaye, W., Treasure, J. and Tyson, E. (2009) "Academy of eating disorders position paper: Eating disorders are serious mental illnesses." *International Journal of Eating Disorders 42,* 2, 97–103.

Lask, B., Britten, C., Kroll, L., Magagna, J. and Tranter, M. (1991) "Children with pervasive refusal." *Archives of Disease in Childhood 66,* 7, 866–869.

Lask, B., and Bryant-Waugh, R. (1993) *Childhood Onset Anorexia Nervosa and Related Eating Disorders.* East Sussex: Lawrence Erlbaum Associates Publishers.

Lask, B., and Bryant-Waugh, R. (2007) "Overview of management." In B. Lask and R. Bryant-Waugh (eds) *Eating Disorders in Childhood and Adolescence* (3rd ed.). London and New York: Routledge Taylor & Francis Group.

Lask, B., Bryant-Waugh, R., Wright, F., Campbell, M., Willoughby, K. and Waller, G. (2005) "Family physician consultation patterns indicate high risk for early-onset anorexia nervosa." *International Journal of Eating Disorders 38,* 269–272.

Levy, R. and Curfman, W.C. (2006) *Anorexia Nervosa.* Omaha, NE: eMedicine. Accessed on 17 March 2009 at http://emedicine.medscape.com.

Lock, J. and LeGrange, D. (2001) "Can family-based treatment of anorexia nervosa be manualized?" *Journal of Psychotherapy Practice and Research 10,* 253–261.

Lock, J. and LeGrange, D. (2005) *Help Your Teenager Beat an Eating Disorder.* New York: The Guilford Press.

Lock, J., Agras, W.S., Bryson, S. and Kraemer, H.C. (2005) "A comparison of short- and long-term family therapy for adolescent anorexia nervosa." *Journal of the American Academy of Child and Adolescent Psychiatry 44,* 7, 632–639.

Lock. J., LeGrange, D., Agras, W.S. and Dare, C. (2001) *Treatment Manual for Anorexia Nervosa.* New York: The Guilford Press.

Miller, J.B. (1991) "The development of women's sense of self." In J.V. Jordan, A.G. Kaplan, J.B. Miller, I.P. Stiver and J.L. Surrey (eds) *Women's Growth in Connection.* New York: The Guilford Press.

Morris, A. (2001) "The medical assessment of anorexia nervosa." *The Clinician 2,* 2, 24–28.

Nasser, M., Katzman, M.A. and Gordon, R.A. (eds) (2001) *Eating Disorders and Cultures in Transition.* New York: Taylor & Francis Inc.

National Collaborating Centre for Mental Health and National Institute for Clinical Excellence (2004) *Eating Disorders: Core Interventions in the Treatment and Management of Anorexia Nervosa, Bulimia Nervosa and Related Eating Disorders.* Leicester and London: The British Psychological Society and the Royal College of Psychiatrists.

National Women's Health Information Center, U.S. Department of Health and Human Services, Office on Women's Health (2006) *Frequently Asked Questions: Anorexia Nervosa.* Washington, DC: National Women's Health Information Center, U.S. Department of Health and Human Services, Office on Women's Health. Accessed on 26 April 2009 at www.womenshealth.gov.

Nunn, K., Frampton, I., Gordon, I. and Lask, B. (2008) "The fault is not in her parents but in her insula – a neurobiological hypothesis of anorexia nervosa." *European Eating Disorders Review 16,* 355–360.

Oldershaw, A., Hambrook, D., Stahl, D., Tchanturiak, K., Treasure, J. and Schmidt, U. (2011) "The socio-emotional processing stream in anorexia nervosa." *Neuroscience and Biobehavioural Reviews 35,* 970–988.

Piran, N. (2005) "Prevention of eating disorders: A review of outcome evaluation research." *Israel Journal of Psychiatry and Related Sciences 42,* 3, 172–177.

Piran, N. and Thompson, S. (2008) "A study of the adverse social experiences model to the development of eating disorders." *International Journal of Health Promotion and Education 46,* 2, 65–71.

Prochaska, J.O., Norcross, J.C. and Diclemente, C.C. (1995) *Changing For Good.* New York: Avon Books Inc.

Puxley, F., Midtsund, M., Iosif, A. and Lask, B. (2008) "PANDAS anorexia nervosa – endangered, extinct, or nonexistent?" *International Journal of Eating Disorders 41,* 15–21.

Roberts, M.E., Tchanturia, K., Stahl, D., Southgate, L. and Treasure, J. (2007) "A systematic review and meta-analysis of set-shifting ability in eating disorders." *Psychological Medicine 37*, 1075–1084.

Rome, E.S., Ammerman, S., Rosen, D.S., Keller, R.J., *et al.* (2003) "Children and adolescents with eating disorders: The state of the art." *Pediatrics 111*, e98–e108.

Rudy, L.J. (2006) *Refrigerator Mothers*. New York: About.com. Accessed on 17 April 2009 at www.autism.about.com.

Scholz, M., Rix, M., Scholz, K., Gantchev, K. and Thomke, V. (2005) "Multiple family therapy for anorexia nervosa: Concepts, experiences and results." *Journal of Family Therapy 27*, 132–141.

Sidiropoulos, M. (2007) "Anorexia nervosa: The physiological consequences of starvation and the need for primary prevention efforts." *McGill Journal of Medicine 10*, 1, 20–25.

Slater, A. and Tiggemann, M. (2002) "A test of objectification theory in adolescent girls." *Sex Roles: A Journal of Research 46*, 9–10, 343–349.

Strober, M., Freeman, R. and Morrell, W. (1997) "The long-term course of severe anorexia nervosa in adolescents: Survival analysis of recovery, relapse, and outcome predictors over 10–15 years in a prospective study." *International Journal of Eating Disorders 22*, 339–360.

Tyron, W.W. (2005) "Possible mechanisms for why desensitization and exposure therapy work." *Clinical Psychology Review 25*, 1, 67–95.

Weiner, R.C. (1999) "Working with physicians toward the goal of primary and secondary prevention." In N. Piran, M. Levine and C. Steiner-Adair (eds) *Preventing Eating Disorders: A Handbook of Interventions and Special Challenges*. Ann Arbor, MI: Taylor & Francis.

Woodside, B. (2007) "Medical complications and prognosis in anorexia nervosa." PowerPoint presentation at the Hospital for Sick Children, Toronto, May 24.

World Health Organization (2007) *International Classification of Diseases and Related Health Problems (10th Revision)*. Geneva: World Health Organization. Accessed on 24 June 2011 at http://apps.who.int/classifications/apps/icd/icd10online.

Zastrow, A., Kaiser, S., Stippich, C., Walther, S., *et al.* (2009) "Neural correlates of impaired cognitive-behavioural flexibility in anorexia nervosa." *American Journal of Psychiatry 166*, 608–616.

Zipfel, S., Reas, D.L., Thornton, C., Olmsted, M.P., *et al.* (2002) "Day hospitalization programs for eating disorders: A systematic review of the literature." *International Journal of Eating Disorders 31*, 2, 105–117.

Subject Index

Author Index